One Thousand Years with Jesus

One Thousand Years with Jesus

The Coming Messianic Kingdom

MATTHEW BRYCE ERVIN

Foreword by Michael L. Brown

RESOURCE *Publications* • Eugene, Oregon

ONE THOUSAND YEARS WITH JESUS
The Coming Messianic Kingdom

Resource Publications
An Imprint of Wipf and Stock Publishers
199 W. 8th Ave., Suite 3
Eugene, OR 97401

www.wipfandstock.com

PAPERBACK ISBN: 978-1-5326-1071-4
HARDCOVER ISBN: 978-1-5326-1073-8
EBOOK ISBN: 978-1-5326-1072-1

Manufactured in the U.S.A.   FEBRUARY 14, 2017

For
Kenneth & Betty

Contents

CONTENTS

Foreword

PREACHING SHORTLY AFTER THE crucifixion and resurrection of Jesus, Peter tells his Jewish listeners that if they will repent, God will send the Messiah back to earth, since heaven must receive him "until the time for restoring all the things about which God spoke by the mouth of his holy prophets long ago" (Acts 3:21, ESV). And so, in one clear sentence, Peter tells us that everything the prophets spoke of in the past, including all the promises to Israel about the Messiah's glorious rule on the earth, will come to pass when King Jesus returns. So much for the New Testament "spiritualizing" away the promises of the Old Testament.

It is true, of course, that the New Testament authors frequently make spiritual applications based on the teachings of the Hebrew Scriptures (also known as the Old Testament, but simply "the Scriptures" to first century Jews). But in doing so, they do not nullify the plain sense of those teachings, since to do so would be to rob those scriptures of their fundamental meaning and to make the sky the limit in terms of how those sacred writings should be understood. Clearly in Acts 3:21, Peter is reiterating that the time will come for the "restoration of all things" (NKJV), as spoken by Israel's prophets, and in this book, Matthew Ervin does an excellent job of laying out just what those prophets promised, as reaffirmed by the New Testament writers. His thesis is simple: What the Bible repeatedly states will happen in the future will happen in the future. It's that simple.

Of course, when it comes to eschatology, it is impossible (and unwise) to be dogmatic on every point, and here in particular we do not want to divide over our differences. Every eschatological system—from historic premillennialism, which is advocated here, to the more recent dispensational premillennialism, and from amillennialism to postmillennialism—has certain "problem verses" that seem to challenge the coherence of that system. Nonetheless, it is fair to ask, if you could read the Bible fluently in the original languages, and if you could be isolated for a period of years, reading through that Bible over and over again, would you end up believing what you believe today? Would you hold to your current doctrinal and eschatological systems or would you conclude that some of what you were taught was based on human tradition more than on Scripture itself?

As a fairly new believer, I became extremely hungry for God's Word, reading the Scriptures two hours a day and memorizing verses one hour a day (I was able to memorize twenty verses a day at that time, meaning that after six months, I had memorized more than 3,600 verses). If you asked me to defend what I believed, I would quote multiple verses back to you, often in machine gun style. (While I was admittedly weak on compassion and wisdom in those days, just seventeen-years-old and newly saved from two years of heavy drug use, I was certainly not weak on zeal!)

One day a friend asked me about details of the second coming of Jesus—based on the way it was taught in our home church—and I told him, "I don't know much about the subject." Determined to make up for this, I devoured a number of recommended books until I had mastered the system and could shoot down any objections. Then it dawned on me one day that I had never seen this intricate, end-time scheme when reading the Bible for myself. I had to learn it from others. In contrast, every other point of doctrine I held to I was able to defend from Scripture, based on immersing myself in the Word.

To be clear, I am not claiming doctrinal infallibility or asserting that everything I believe is beyond the pale of criticism, and I am not minimizing the importance of corporate study and learning. I'm simply saying that I realized which doctrines could be readily deduced through an inductive reading of the Word and which doctrines could not. Eventually, when I restudied the second coming of the Lord, I abandoned the system I was taught in my church, realizing that it was, in my opinion, lacking in biblical foundations.

The question at hand, then, is this: Would a person become a premillennialist based on an exhaustive, repeated study of the Scriptures? An amillennialist? A postmillennialist? That is where the real debate lies, and while we do well not to divide over eschatology, it is still worth asking: If I never heard of any of these systems of thought and I read the Bible cover to cover, inductively and deductively, would I expect a literal, divine kingdom on the earth when Jesus returns, a kingdom with Israel at the center of it? I personally believe the answer is yes, although again, I do not judge the sincerity or devotion or scholarship of those who differ with me on this point. I simply believe, after more than forty-five years of reading the Scriptures, that this is the most natural interpretation of the cumulative biblical witness. It was also the most widely-held belief among the disciples of the apostles, as Matthew ably demonstrates towards the end of this book.

May I encourage you to test this out as you read the pages that follow? With each text cited, ask yourself, "Is Matthew treating this text fairly? Is he reading something into the text that is not there, or is he letting the text speak for itself? Is he forcing a presupposed understanding onto the text, or is he deducing his understanding from the text? And would the authors of scripture be surprised at his handling of what they wrote or would they likely affirm it as what they intended to say?"

What might be eye-opening to readers who do not hold to a premillennial reading of the Scriptures is: 1) just how many verses speak to the issue of the Messiah's future, earthly reign, the coming kingdom of God; and 2) just how much the New Testament writers reinforce that vision rather than negate it or modify it. Yes, Jesus the Messiah will return, and He will reign from Jerusalem for 1,000 years before we enter God's eternal, perfect kingdom.

Does that earthly kingdom represent a step back from Jesus' atoning death on the cross? Why would it? Jesus is the both the Messiah of Israel and the Savior of the world (in reality, He is the latter only because He is the former), and He did not come to abolish the Torah *or the prophets* (Matthew 5:17) but rather to fulfill. We are saved from sin by His death, and when He returns, He will resurrect us and we will reign together with Him as God fulfills the words of the prophets.

As for the presence of animal sacrifices in the future millennial Temple—often *the* greatest stumbling block to belief in premillennialism—Matthew's approach is again straightforward. First, he argues that it is not just Ezekiel who speaks of future sacrifices (in the midst of chs. 40–48) but Isaiah, Jeremiah, Zechariah, and Malachi as well. Second, he points out that animal sacrifices could never do what the cross does, and so whatever role they will have in the future (memorial or other) in no way will it compete with, minimize, or negate the finality of Jesus' atoning death.

Is there room for debate on these issues? Of course there is. But, to say it again, what many readers will be find eye-opening is the consistency of the biblical witness on some of these controversial subjects. Did the prophets mean what they said literally, or is their meaning to be entirely spiritualized in passage after passage?

As for the concept of realized eschatology—also known as "already-not-yet"—I do believe the New Testament clearly teaches that, in some sense, the rule of God (= the kingdom of God) has broken powerfully into this age, and that kingdom advances wherever the gospel drives back the powers of darkness (see, e.g., Luke 10:8–9). There are some entirely spiritual dimensions to God's kingdom that can be enjoyed in the here and now (Romans 14:17). Yet the very fact that we still pray for the coming of the kingdom and for God's will to be done on earth as it is in heaven (Matthew 6:9–13) reminds us that, in a very real sense, the kingdom has *not yet* come. Moreover, it is clear that many of the words of the prophets describing the Lord's beatific kingdom have not yet come to pass. As Professor D. A. Carson noted in his commentary on Matthew in the *Expositor's Bible Commentary*, whoever reads the words of the Lord's Prayer in Matthew's Gospel "perceives that the kingdom has already broken in and *prays for its extension as well as for its unqualified manifestation*" (my emphasis). It is the purpose of this book to explore the kingdom of God in "its unqualified manifestation" and to challenge each reader to examine the scriptural evidence afresh.

One last note. Many critics of premillennialism, which has as its unshakable foundation the veracity of God's promises to Israel, reject this system because they associate it with dispensationalism, a more recent teaching that was unknown to the early Church. The reader should know that there is not a syllable in this book that requires the embrace of a pretribulational rapture or any other dispensational distinctives. The premillennial eschatological system must be evaluated on its own merits, and here, in clear and readable language, Matthew Ervin has set forth the scriptural merits of that system for all to examine and weigh. May we follow the truth of Scripture wherever it leads.

Michael L. Brown, PhD

1

The Time is Coming

THE TIME IS COMING when the world will be radically changed for the better. It will last for a thousand years, bookended by resurrections, first of the just and then of the unjust. Satan will be chained in the abyss, no longer free to influence the nations. The saints will reign alongside the King of kings, Jesus Christ. This is a time that will begin after the return of the Messiah and end with Satan's total defeat and the judgment of sinners. It is the very culmination of history, a transition away from the fallen world into the perfection of the Eternal State. This is a time known as the Millennium. These distinctives make up what is referred to as Premillennialism, meaning that the Messiah must return before the commencement of the thousand years. Those who affirm this doctrine are called premillennialists. This future era was known by the Hebrews as the Messianic Age and the Messianic Kingdom.

The cardinal passage on the Millennium is Revelation 20:1–7:

> Then I saw an angel coming down from heaven, holding in his hand the key to the bottomless pit and a great chain. And he seized the dragon, that ancient serpent, who is the devil and Satan, and bound him for a thousand years, and threw him into the pit, and shut it and sealed it over him, so that he might not deceive the nations any longer, until the thousand years were ended. After that he must be released for a little while. Then I saw thrones, and seated on them were those to whom the authority to judge was committed. Also I saw the souls of those who had been beheaded for the testimony of Jesus and for the word of God, and those who had not worshiped the beast or its image and had not received its mark on their foreheads or their hands. They came to life and reigned with Christ for a thousand years. The rest of the dead did not come to life until the

thousand years were ended. This is the first resurrection. Blessed and holy is the one who shares in the first resurrection! Over such the second death has no power, but they will be priests of God and of Christ, and they will reign with him for a thousand years. And when the thousand years are ended, Satan will be released from his prison

The thousand years are mentioned six times in just seven verses. The specificity of the span of time is Revelation 20's greatest contribution to our knowledge of the Millennial Kingdom.[1] There is, however, a common misconception that this passage is the only place in the Bible where the Millennium is taught. In reality, it is a summary of what can be found woven throughout all of Scripture.

An understanding of the Millennium makes the Bible come together as one metanarrative. It helps tell the story of the Scriptures. Otherwise difficult passages become easier to understand and place in the prophetic timeline. God has made promises in his unconditional covenants, many of which will be fulfilled in the Millennium. Israel will finally realize her destiny as the head the nations, in the midst of a world moving toward Eden. Resurrected saints, including some of the most remarkable from Scripture, will hold high offices with responsibilities to match as they reign under King Jesus. Jerusalem will be the capital of the world on the same summit where the Messiah's home, a massive temple with miracles flowing forth, will also sit. As incredible as these things are, the main point of the Millennium is the exaltation of the Lord Jesus. His kingdom will be demonstrated in contradistinction to an unbelieving world, proving once and for all which is superior. The saved and the unsaved alike will behold the Messiah's rightful place as the divine sovereign of the universe.

INTERPRETING THE MILLENNIUM

Hermeneutics is the science of interpretation, especially of Scripture. Use of the proper hermeneutic is especially important in understanding prophecy. Virtually all of the major disagreements on prophetic passages can be traced back to different methods of interpretation. The hermeneutic applied in this book is the literal, grammatical, and historical. It is literal in that the words on the page are understood according to their ordinary and plain meaning. This means that exegesis is of paramount importance

---

1. Though not explicitly stated, the duration of the Millennium may be implied in Psalm 90:4 and in 2 Peter 3:8.

while eisegesis must be shunned. Exegesis means to extract from or take something out, resulting in the reader being informed by the text. Eisegesis means to bring something in and impose it upon the text, resulting in it being manipulated to mean something that the words and context in themselves were never intended to convey. Being grammatical means that the grammar and context are strictly observed and unpacked. How words and their definitions, phrases, and sentences relate to one another are carefully examined. The historical part of the hermeneutic requires that the reader be mindful of the original audience and historical setting. *The interpreter should, therefore, endeavour to take himself from the present, and to transport himself into the historical position of his author, look through his eyes, note his surroundings, feel with his heart, and catch his emotion. Herein we note the import of the term grammatico-historical interpretation.*[2] The literal, grammatical, and historical hermeneutic is often referred to simply as the literal hermeneutic for short.

Use of this hermeneutic is only common sense as God meant for his word to be understood. He would not have sought to deceive his audience (cf. Num 23:19; Heb 6:17–18). It was Satan who first responded to God's clear word by asking, *did God actually say?* (Gen 3:1). A legitimate interpretation can never be so far from the plain meaning that it requires special insight or extra-biblical sources to decipher. Thus, the literal hermeneutic is materially inseparable from Sola Scriptura. Deviation from the method often leads to as many different interpretations as there are interpreters. All one has to do is look at a few different non-literal commentaries on the meaning of passages such as Isaiah 11, Ezekiel 47, or Zechariah 14 to witness the absolute lack of conformity. In contrast, the literal commentaries are strikingly consistent with one another.

Just because the correct hermeneutic is literal in the overall approach, it does not mean that everything is to be taken literally. No one reading the Scriptures at face value would think that Jesus has hinges because he is the door (John 10:9) or that he has leaves just because he is the true vine (John 15:1). Nevertheless, critics of Premillennialism often accuse its professors of taking Scripture too literally. *The simple truth is, that not a single Millenarian author, from the days of the apostles down, holds to such an opinion; all of them, without exception, fully recognize symbols, types, and figures of speech, notice their peculiarities, and discriminate them from the strictly literal.*[3] We

2. Terry, *Biblical Hermeneutics*, 231.
3. Peters, *Theocratic Kingdom*, 63.

are often told what various symbols mean elsewhere in the given book. For example, in Daniel 7 the prophet received a symbolic vision of four beasts. Later in the same chapter, the meaning of the symbols are interpreted. The book of Revelation is filled with symbols, and it is clear when they are in use. The text either directly tells us what the symbols mean (e.g., Rev 1:16, 20) or they are borrowed from earlier prophecies with which the original audience was well acquainted. Using Scripture to interpret itself, including symbols, illustrations, and figures of speech, is an important part of the literal hermeneutic.

Perhaps the greatest virtue of the literal hermeneutic is that it leads to genuine knowledge of the spiritual. Scripture has a spiritual meaning only because it has a literal meaning. Spiritual blessings came from Jesus' literal death on the cross and from his literal resurrection. To ignore the plain meaning of the text in favor of a hidden "spiritual" one prevents actual spiritual truths from being learned.

The True Prophet Rule

It is the literal hermeneutic that is prescribed in Scripture. This can be gleaned from a few places, most notably in Deuteronomy 18:21–22:

> And if you say in your heart, 'How may we know the word that the LORD has not spoken?'-when a prophet speaks in the name of the LORD, if the word does not come to pass or come true, that is a word that the LORD has not spoken; the prophet has spoken it presumptuously. You need not be afraid of him.

Prophets were exposed as being false when what they prophesied did not come to pass. These false prophets could not explain away their failures by identifying them as mere allegories or nebulous spiritualized messages. False prophets were so harmful that they were to be executed (Deut 18:20; cf. 13:1–5). If a prophetic word actually came from the LORD then it would be fulfilled just as reported. This is the seal of approval upon a true prophet. Surely God holds himself to the same, or a higher standard than what he places upon his prophets. If the LORD says something is his word, then we should expect it to mean just what it says it does according to a normal reading. This is the true prophet rule of interpretation. Its consistent application reveals incredible and awe-inspiring facts about the Millennium.

2

The Promises of God

THE FOUNDATION FOR ESCHATOLOGY must be identified and understood before the necessity for the Millennium can be fully appreciated. This foundation consists of God's unconditional covenants with some of the Bible's most important patriarchs and Israel. Covenants are usually thought of as agreements between two parties. If one party is negligent in fulfilling what was agreed upon, the other party is free to renege. However, in Scripture we often read of covenants where God shows fidelity even if those on the other end do not. This is rather intriguing as God would be fully justified in abandoning his responsibilities once a covenant is broken. Nevertheless, God is faithful even when his people are not.

Contracts in which God agrees to keep his end of the agreement even if the other party does not are understood as unconditional covenants. These covenants may include some conditions but they are not able to prevent what God says that he will do. Simply put, unconditional covenants are fundamentally promises or a collection of promises. When God makes a promise he always keeps it. If God did not keep his promises it would mean that he is a liar. It is both axiomatic and a plain teaching from Scripture to say that God would never lie (Titus 1:2; Heb 6:18). Though a thorough survey of the unconditional covenants cannot be included, highlights are necessary to fully appreciate later chapters.

GOD MADE A PROMISE TO ABRAHAM

The nature of the Abrahamic Covenant is strikingly unconditional as recorded in the ceremony of Genesis 15:7–12 and 15:17–18:

> And he said to him, "I am the LORD who brought you out from Ur of the Chaldeans to give you this land to possess." But he said, "O Lord God, how am I to know that I shall possess it?" He said to him, "Bring me a heifer three years old, a female goat three years old, a ram three years old, a turtledove, and a young pigeon." And he brought him all these, cut them in half, and laid each half over against the other. But he did not cut the birds in half. And when birds of prey came down on the carcasses, Abram drove them away. As the sun was going down, a deep sleep fell on Abram. And behold, dreadful and great darkness fell upon him.
>
> When the sun had gone down and it was dark, behold, a smoking fire pot and a flaming torch passed between these pieces. On that day the LORD made a covenant with Abram, saying, "To your offspring I give this land, from the river of Egypt to the great river, the river Euphrates,

This corridor of slain animals seems strange to the modern mind, though it would have been understood as the norm during Abraham's time. The most notable difference here is that five animals[1] are used instead of the standard one. God was amplifying the already severe commitment to be made by anyone passing through the animals. The cutting of these animals into halves contributes to the *cutting of the covenant*, as it was referred to in more ancient times. By cutting these animals, the parties entering into the covenant are saying that if they break the agreement they shall likewise be severed. Compare this ceremony to the one in Jeremiah 34:18–20. There we learn of various leaders and people in the land that entered into a covenant by passing through the halves of a calf. They did not honor their commitments, and so God handed them over to their enemies, their bodies to be feasted upon by birds and beasts. While breaking a covenant may not have resulted in the participants literally being cut in half, there were clearly dire consequences to be faced.

---

1. The turtledove and young pigeon were not cut in half. Apparently this was the standard practice when dealing with these birds (Lev 1:14–17). Mary and Joseph sacrificed a pair of turtledoves or two young pigeons when they presented Jesus to the Lord (Luke 2:22–24).

With the serious nature of a blood covenant in mind it becomes all the more remarkable to see that it is the LORD alone who moved between the rows of animal halves. The smoking furnace and flaming torch describe how he appeared. The covenant would have still been unconditional had Abram opted out or fallen asleep on his own. It is even more profound that the LORD caused Abram to fall asleep (v. 12). God determined that he alone would be the one to carry the full weight of the covenant. The LORD bound himself and so he must stay true to what he has promised Abram. Because the LORD completed the ceremony without Abram, God must honor his commitments. Nothing that Abram and his descendants did or will do can change that.

A Delayed Fulfillment

The birds of prey coming down upon the carcasses and Abram driving them away in Genesis 15:11 might have been mentioned for posterity, though the incident likely holds some illustrative significance. The promises God made to Abram contained an element of delay: the enslavement of the Hebrews by the Egyptians. This is confirmed in Genesis 15:13–16. The sojourning of the Hebrews in a land not their own was initially in Canaan, though the majority of time was spent in Egypt. The four hundred year affliction delayed the Hebrews experiencing God's promises. Even now the promises have not been fully realized. The pattern of the Jewish people being imprisoned and dispersed form their land has continued throughout history.

Birds can represent satanic activity; Jesus used birds as a picture for Satan (Mark 4:4, 15). It is reasonable to speculate that the birds represent the same in Genesis 15:11. The bondage of the Hebrews is itself not a promise in the same sense, but part of the reality of waiting for all of God's promises to reach their final and complete state. God may make promises but he will act on them according to his own timetable. That timetable requires the remnant of Israel coming to know Jesus as the Messiah before the promises can be fully experienced (cf. Isa 10:20–22; Hos 5:15; Matt 23:39). Abram drove the birds away and the partial hardening currently affecting the people of Israel will also be removed (Rom 11:25–27). This will be followed by the Millennium, during which God will finally give all that he has promised to Abraham.

Details of the Abrahamic Covenant

The details of the covenant are found in Genesis 12:1–3:

> Now the LORD said to Abram, "Go from your country and your
> kindred and your father's house to the land that I will show you.
> And I will make of you a great nation, and I will bless you and make
> your name great, so that you will be a blessing. I will bless those who
> bless you, and him who dishonors you I will curse, and in you all the
> families of the earth shall be blessed."

There are three distinct promises made by God to Abram. The first is that
God will give Abram and his descendants a very particular piece of land.
God called Abram out of Ur of the Chaldees in Mesopotamia and determined that he would live in what is rightfully referred to as the Promised
Land (cf. Acts 7:2–7). In Genesis 15:18–21 its dimensions are given: from
the river of Egypt (the Nile) to the Euphrates. This is important to remember. Those with an agenda to undermine the Millennium will often attack
its roots. One of the most important roots is this covenant promise regarding the Promised Land. The Bible is very clear that the Promised Land is
on earth and its borders are well defined. It should never be equated with
Heaven or an after-life paradise. It is true that a better country and city has
been prepared for God's people (Heb 11:16). However, this is the heavenly
Jerusalem that will be let down after the Millennium has ended (Heb 12:22;
Rev 21:2).

Abraham only ever dwelled in the land that was given to him. He
and his immediate descendants lived in tents (Heb 11:9). And while God
kept his promise to give the Hebrews the land of Canaan (Gen 17:8; Josh
21:43–45), they have yet to fully inhabit and control the larger territory
(Gen 15:18–21) forevermore (e.g., Gen 17:8; Jer 16:15; Ezek 37:25; Amos
9:15). It is during the Millennium when Abraham and his descendants will
enjoy absolute control of the entire Promised Land.

The next promise made to Abraham is that God will make of him a
great nation. It is explained in Genesis 13:14–16. In addition to affirming
the land promise, we are also provided with further proof that the land was
to belong to Abraham's descendants. Abraham was not just promised some
descendants, but so many that they would be as difficult to count as the dust
of the earth and the stars in the heavens (Gen 15:5; 22:17; cf. Heb 11:12).
Keep in mind that when Abraham was given this promise he was without
children and seventy-five years of age (Gen 12:4). The promise is further

clarified in Genesis 17:6. Here we see that Abraham was to be the father of a multitude of nations.[2] Included among those who make up these nations are kings, including the King of kings, Jesus Christ. All informed children of God believe that this promise means exactly what it says and that it is everlasting. However, many of these same believers refuse to acknowledge that the land promise means what it says or that it was to last forever. The Abrahamic Covenant comes as a package deal. You either believe the covenant as a whole or you must abandon it entirely if you wish to be at all consistent.

The last promise in the Abrahamic Covenant is of blessing. We see that how one treats Abraham, and by extension his promised descendants, results in likewise treatment. To bless Abraham is to receive a blessing, with the same arrangement applied to curses. All of the families of the earth were to be blessed through Abraham. This sublimely came to pass when Abraham's descendant, Jesus, provided for the salvation of Jews and Gentiles alike (cf. Gal 3:14).

It must be stressed that the Abrahamic Covenant is unconditional. The very language God used when reaffirming the Covenant to Isaac emphasized his intention. Count how often *I will* and *will* are used in Genesis 26:3–4:

> Sojourn in this land, and I will be with you and will bless you, for to you and to your offspring I will give all these lands, and I will establish the oath that I swore to Abraham your father. I will multiply your offspring as the stars of heaven and will give to your offspring all these lands. And in your offspring all the nations of the earth shall be blessed.

The phrase *I will* is used four times, with the word *will* being used a total of six times in just these two verses.[3] In comparison, God never says *if* or requires something of Isaac, other than to simply dwell in the land that was given. In Genesis alone, the Abrahamic Covenant is affirmed yet again with God repeating the promises to Jacob (Gen 28:14–15). When a teacher repeats him or herself even once, the wise student will make sure to pay

2. The nations are those springing from Abraham's sons Isaac (Gen 17:19) and Ishmael (Gen 17:20). The children of Abraham's wife Keturah also formed nations (Gen 25:1–4), though of less prominence. The blessing of Abraham has come to believing Gentiles (Gal 3:14).

3. The repetition of *I will* and *will* as said by God are common in the unconditional covenants.

attention. When God repeats himself multiple times, it is all the more critical that what he says be taken seriously.

Awaiting Fulfillment

God has already honored many aspects of the promises that he made to Abraham. Abraham was absolutely blessed spiritually (e.g., Gen 14:19; 21:22). The patriarch was certainly given many nations, and in ways that he did not likely imagine (cf. Matt 3:9). In Abraham, all the families of the earth were blessed by his descendant Jesus (e.g., Gal 3:8, 16). Nevertheless, this does not mean that the covenant has completed its work. Neither Abraham nor his descendants have ever fully possessed the Promised Land, let alone doing so forever (Gen 13:15; 17:8).

The psalmist summarized and emphasized the eternality of the covenant promise regarding the land in Psalm 105:7–11:

> He is the LORD our God; his judgments are in all the earth. He remembers his covenant forever, the word that he commanded, for a thousand generations, the covenant that he made with Abraham, his sworn promise to Isaac, which he confirmed to Jacob as a statute, to Israel as an everlasting covenant, saying, "To you I will give the land of Canaan as your portion for an inheritance."

After reading this, can anyone who claims to trust in Scripture honestly doubt that the Jewish people have a divine right to the Promised Land? Could Scripture somehow be any clearer in conveying this truth? We can be assured that our God is a God that keeps his promises and is faithful to his word.

Even at this point the nation of Israel has only been partially restored. The descendants of Abraham, through Isaac and then Jacob, now both dwell in and control some of the Promised Land. The majority of the land is yet to fall under Jewish control. Furthermore, the Jews are experiencing occupation by those worshipping a false god on the Temple Mount. The land promise in the Abrahamic Covenant has not been completed. If those things that are either directly promised by God or originate from those promises have not yet occurred, then we must conclude that they will in the future. Israel will be in a position to bless the world more than ever before in the Millennium.

A PROMISED LAND

The unconditional covenant covered here is commonly referred to as the *Palestinian Covenant*. This is a misnomer of the highest order, rooted in anti-Semitism. The Roman Emperor Hadrian renamed Judea *Palaestina*, from which *Palestine* is derived, in an attempt to erase the Hebrew claim to the land in 135 AD. In recent history the designation has become incorrectly associated more with Arabs than it is with Jews. It is for this very reason that theologians like Arnold Fruchtenbaum prefer the name, *the Land Covenant*.[4] Fruchtenbaum is to be highly commended for seeking to break free from an error based on habit. This author prefers to go one step further and use the name, *the Promised Land Covenant*. This emphasizes the fundamental nature behind the Hebrew's claim to the land via God's promises. Even believers, and many who are not, with only a little knowledge of Scripture have heard of the Promised Land.

The Promised Land Covenant is an amplification of the land promise in the Abrahamic Covenant. It is recorded in Deuteronomy 29:1—30:10 and is made between God and Israel. Moses made it clear that the Promised Land Covenant is distinct from the Mosaic Covenant (29:1). This distinction underscores that none should perceive the Promised Land Covenant as being conditional due to wrongly grouping it with the Mosaic.[5] The Hebrews had to obey God's voice and meet their obligations in order to obtain the blessings of the Mosaic Covenant (Exod 19:5). This is not the case with the Promised Land Covenant, made clear by the identification of its clauses.

Moses reminded the people of the great trials, signs, and wonders that they had witnessed. The LORD had not given the people the heart to understand what he had done for them (29:4). As a result, the first clause was the act of God uprooting the Hebrews from their land (29:28). The remaining clauses concern the reversal of the first. The people will be enabled to appreciate what God has done for them and they will return to him (30:2). God promised that he would ingather the Hebrews back into the Promised Land (Deut 30:3–4; cf. Hos 11:10–11; Mark 13:26–27).

God made some additional promises in Deuteronomy 30:5–9:

> And the LORD your God will bring you into the land that your fathers possessed, that you may possess it. And he will make you more

---

4. Fruchtenbaum, *Israelology*, 581.

5. Paul similarly contrasted the temporary nature of the Mosaic Covenant with the eternal nature of the Abrahamic Covenant (Gal 3:15–20).

prosperous and numerous than your fathers. And the LORD your
God will circumcise your heart and the heart of your offspring, so
that you will love the LORD your God will all your heart and will all
your soul, that you may live. And the LORD your God will put all
these curses on your foes and enemies who persecuted you. And you
shall again obey the voice of the LORD and keep all his command-
ments that I commanded you today. The LORD your God will make
you abundantly prosperous in all the work of your hand, in the fruit
of your womb and in the fruit of your cattle and in the fruit of your
ground. For the LORD will again take delight in prospering you, as
he took delight in your fathers,

Not only will God bring the Hebrews back into their land, but he promised
to make the future inhabitants more prosperous than their ancestors (v. 5).
This promise will be completely realized during the millennial reign of Jesus. The Messianic Kingdom's inauguration follows two prerequisites. First,
God promised to perform a work of grace in the hearts of the Hebrews.
This will enable them to truly love God, obey him, and live (v. 6). Second,
the LORD will punish Israel's enemies (v. 7; cf. Joel 3:2; Zech 14:12). He
will then bless the Hebrews with an abundance of children, animals, and
produce from the land (v. 9; cf. Amos 9:13–15). This last promise will be
fulfilled during the Millennium and speaks to the very nature of that age.

The Unfaithful Bride

Ezekiel 16 contains the parable of the adulterous bride. Unfortunately, this
is an all too common description of Israel (e.g., Isa 1:21; 50:1; Jer 2; Hos
1–3). The narrative is intended to remind Israel of her sins and the blessings that she is nevertheless due. Israel's genealogical origin is described in
a way that speaks to her morality (v. 3). She was said to be born out of the
Amorites and the Hittites, pagan nations. With the later, Ezekiel seemed
to be suggesting that it is inherent to Israel's nature to be adulterous. Her
adultery was evidenced by her various sordid relationships with other gods,
idols, and countries (vv. 26–29).

Israel is depicted as an infant that was neglected and cast out into a
field (vv. 16:4–6). The LORD declared that this fledgling nation was to live
and he proceeded to greatly increase their numbers (vv. 6–7). Now that
Israel had matured she was taken as the LORD's bride (vv. 8–14). However,
Israel's adultery was of such magnitude and enormity that it warranted extensive treatment by Ezekiel (vv. 15–34). The nation was engaged in truly

horrific acts as part of her adultery. Included among them was the demonic practice of sacrificing infant children to the pagan god Molech (vv. 20–21). As just punishment, the Israelites were cast out and dispersed (vv. 35–52).

When speaking about marriage, even Jesus allowed for divorce in the case of the wife committing adultery (Matt 19:9). Likewise, it would be perfectly reasonable for God to disown Israel. Keep in mind that she had already abandoned the LORD via her embrace of false gods and alliances with pagan countries. Israel even killed her own infant children by burning them to death. It is hard to imagine a husband maintaining fidelity toward a wife that had committed such heinous sins. Thankfully, God's faithfulness is without end or limit. The LORD will restore his bride (vv. 53–63).

The parable of the adulterous bride in Ezekiel 16 illustrates a key factor in how the Promised Land Covenant operates. The Jewish people's actual use of the land is based on their obedience to God. Thus, the Promised Land Covenant does include conditions. However, the covenant as a whole is fundamentally unconditional because Jewish ownership of the Promised Land is based solely on the promise of God. The LORD held up his hand, swearing an oath to give the land to the patriarchs and to the Jews as an inheritance (Ezek 47:14). The time is coming when the Hebrews will enjoy the Promised Land forever because they will be eternally obedient to God. This will be made possible through the people entering into a personal relationship with Jesus the Messiah (Ezek 39:25–29; cf. Zech 12:10).

This directly relates to the reconfirmation of the Promised Land Covenant in Ezekiel 16:60–63:

> yet I will remember my covenant with you in the days of your youth, and I will establish for you an everlasting covenant. Then you will remember your ways and be ashamed when you take your sisters, both your elder and your younger, and I give them to you as daughters, but not on account of the covenant with you, and you shall know that I am the LORD, that you may remember and be confounded, and never open your mouth again because of your shame, when I atone for you all that you have done, declares the Lord God.

As a result of God remembering the Promised Land Covenant,[6] another everlasting covenant is to be established: the New Covenant (v. 60). Israel being brought into the New Covenant will not be due to her obedience to the Mosaic covenant (v. 61). God has already started to bring Jews back

---

6. It is possible that God was referring to the land promise within the Abrahamic Covenant.

into the Promised Land, placing some of it under their control. This has set the stage for the prophesied second return to the land from exile (e.g., Isa 11:11). The LORD will roar like a lion, calling his people home (Hos 11:10–11). Great mercy is being poured out on the Jews even though the vast majority of them reject God and his Son. It was prophesied that only after the Jews had been reestablished in the land that God would make them clean, remove Israel's heart of stone, and replace it with one of flesh (Ezek 36:24–36). Thus, it is precisely because the Jews have begun to return to the land in disbelief that a work of God should be recognized. Because God scattered the Jewish people only he could have regathered them (Zech 10:9–10). When God shuts a door no one else can open it (Rev 3:7).

The Diaspora Continues

The Israelites were returned to their land after the Babylonian captivity in 538 BC (2 Chr 36:22–23; Isa 44:28). It is important to understand that the prophets often wrote about that return as a shadow of a perfect, glorious, permanent, and still future event. It is apparent that the many prophecies typified by Amos 9:15, which calls for an eternal enjoyment of the land, cannot be fulfilled by a temporary habitation. Zechariah penned his prophecies in 518 BC, twenty years after the return from Babylon. And yet, he wrote of another coming exile and return (Zech 10:8–12). The return to the land from the Babylonian captivity simply cannot be understood as the fulfillment of the Promised Land Covenant.

The Jewish people were once again dispersed from their land when the Roman army, under Titus, destroyed the temple and much of Jerusalem in 70 AD. Jesus taught that the scattering of the Jews and the Gentile occupation of the Promised Land, beginning with the destruction of the temple, would only last for a limited period (Luke 21:24).[7] After suffering the atrocities of the Holocaust under Adolf Hitler, the Jews enjoyed the reestablishment of the state of Israel in 1948. Jerusalem was later liberated from Jordanian occupation in 1967 during the Six Day War. Nevertheless, the Jews do not control the vast majority of the Promised Land, extending from the river of Egypt to the Euphrates (Gen 15:18–20). Furthermore, the majority of Jews are still dispersed over the face of the earth. Further

---

7. Note the word *until* in Luke 21:24, signaling an end to the times of the Gentiles and a return to the land by the scattered Jews.

ingathering has yet to occur. Though the principle of firstfruits[8] is in operation, the Promised Land Covenant has not yet been fulfilled. But it will be in the Millennium.

GOD MADE A PROMISE TO DAVID

The Davidic Covenant is comprised of promises made by God to David, making it unconditional. The information most pertinent to understanding the Millennium is first found in 2 Samuel 7:10–13:

> *And I will appoint a place for my people Israel and will plant them, so that they may dwell in their own place and be disturbed no more. And violent men shall afflict them no more, as formerly, from the time that I appointed judges over my people Israel. And I will give you rest from all your enemies. Moreover, the LORD declares to you that the LORD will make you a house. When your days are fulfilled and you lie down with your fathers, I will raise up your offspring after you, who shall come from your body, and I will establish his kingdom. He shall build a house for my name, and I will establish the throne of his kingdom forever.*

The first promise is a reaffirmation that the land of Israel would be for the Hebrew people (vv. 10–11). It is to be a land where they will be disturbed no more. Even if the Jews possessed all of the Promised Land, it would be absurd to say they are not disturbed or given rest from their enemies.

David is next promised a house (v. 11). David was denied his desire to build the temple, but God blessed him in a greater way by building from him a royal dynasty. This promise was a recognition of the kingly line belonging to the tribe of Judah that was to bring about the Lion Messiah (Gen 49:9–10; cf. Rev 5:5). The dynasty would begin with David's son Solomon (v. 12). God promised that Solomon would be the one to build the first temple and that the throne of his kingdom will be established forever (v. 13). Solomon did indeed oversee the building of the temple (1 Kgs 6). God kept the first part of his promise regarding Solomon in a real and literal way. Why should anyone expect God to break his word on the second part? God's steadfast love and covenant will stand firm for David; his throne is as eternal as the days of the heavens (Ps 89:28–29). The LORD said that he would not violate this covenant or alter the words of his lips (Ps 89:34). The kingdom ruled from the Davidic throne will continue forever with Jesus as the Monarch.

8. A sample that promises a far greater harvest or realization.

The Unoccupied Davidic Throne

It is common for those who fight against Premillennialism to claim that Jesus is currently sitting on David's throne. This is primarily done by arguing that Jesus' exaltation at the right hand of God (e.g., Acts 2:33) somehow equals him occupying the Davidic throne. Such a claim totally lacks any exegetical support. Indeed, it is clear that this exaltation results in Jesus currently residing at the right hand of God's throne (Heb 12:2). This event was a fulfillment of Psalm 110, which itself makes no mention of David's throne. The very fact that verse 1 teaches that the Messiah will sit on this throne for a limited period means that it cannot possibly be about the Davidic rule, which is eternal. This Psalm describes just what the premillennialist should expect. Jesus is to sit beside his Father until it is time to crush the governments of man and inaugurate the Davidic Kingdom (Ps 110:1–2, 5–6; Matt 22:44). In quoting Amos 9:11–12, James said that the tabernacle of David was yet to be rebuilt from its ruins (Acts 15:15–16). It is clear that James did not believe that Jesus' earlier ascension had restored the tabernacle of David, i.e., the rule of his line.

Even more damaging to the non-premillennialist is that God's word makes it perfectly clear that the Davidic throne, or reign of David's heir, must be on the earth in Jerusalem. There are many passages that prove this. One of the most useful is Psalm 132:11–14:

> The LORD swore to David a sure oath from which he will not turn back: "One of the sons of your body I will set on your throne. If your sons keep my covenant and my testimonies that I shall teach them, their sons also forever shall sit on your throne." For the LORD has chosen Zion; he has desired it for his dwelling place: This is my resting place forever; here I will dwell, for I have desired it.

The student of Scripture does not have to be especially perspicacious to notice that God is serious about fulfilling his promise to David. David's descendants occupied his throne in Jerusalem. God desired the city as his dwelling place and not just for a particular period of time. The LORD equated the throne being occupied forever with him dwelling in Jerusalem forever. The final descendant is he who obeyed the statutes perfectly (Matt 5:17), the horn of David[9] (Ps 132:17), the God-man Jesus. God will most

---

9. The *horn* (Ps 132:17; Ezek 29:21; Luke 1:69) or its synonym the *branch* (Jer 23:5; 33:15; Zech 3:8; 6:12) are kingly messianic titles.

certainly be dwelling in Jerusalem as it will be Jesus who sits on David's throne.

Further evidence of an earthly location includes the need to enter through the gates of Jerusalem to access the throne of David (Jer 17:25). The throne is said to be in Jerusalem in Judah (Jer 22:30), not a vague heavenly location. The reign of the Messiah on David's throne is for the purpose of ruling over all of the earth and executing judgment upon it (Jer 23:5–6; cf. Zech 14:9). Because the Messiah's rule from David's throne is from Jerusalem on earth, the reign cannot currently be taking place. Jesus even said that man is not in a position to know when the kingdom would be restored to Israel (Acts 1:6–7).

While this evidence should more than suffice to prove that Jesus is yet to sit on the Davidic throne, one final passage should remove any lingering doubt. Revelation 3:21:

> The one who conquers, I will grant him to sit with me on my throne,
> as I also conquered and sat down with my Father on his throne.

The Messiah was clearly speaking of two distinct thrones. Jesus referred to the throne that those who conquer are to share with him in the future as *my throne*. This is in contrast to the Father's throne that Jesus sat down on after he conquered. Surely the later throne is to be associated with the exaltation of Christ (cf. Acts 2:33; Heb 12:2) and not the former. Consider that if the two thrones being spoken of are one in the same then that would mean that the Davidic throne was established before David was even created. This cannot be the case as God promised David that the throne would be (future tense) established (2 Sam 7:16).

The described earthly throne in the promise to David currently has no occupant. As such, it can be asserted that there is one yet to come. The King who is to rule forever is Jesus Christ. After Gabriel informed Mary that she was to bear a son to be named Jesus, she is told the following in Luke 1:32–33:

> He will be great and will be called the Son of the Most High. And
> the Lord God will give to him the throne of his father David, and he
> will reign over the house of Jacob forever, and of his kingdom there
> will be no end."

The proper biblical concept of the kingdom necessarily includes Jesus reigning from David's throne. David being referred to as Jesus' father is especially telling. Jesus identified himself as the Messiah by connecting it to him being the Son of David (e.g., Mark 12:35–37). Many people did not hesitate to call Jesus the Son of David out of recognition that he was the Messiah (e.g., Matt 1:1; 15:22; 20:30; Mark 10:47). When the Pharisees heard Jesus being honored in this manner they became indignant (Matt 21:15). What they all understood was that the title *Son of David* referred to the one who would establish David's throne forever (2 Sam 7:16).

All true Christians, by definition, confess that Jesus is the Messiah in reference to him being God and Savior (e.g., Rom 10:9). Surely then, other definitions regarding the full person of the Messiah should also be accepted. Jesus is the Son of David and therefore must fulfill the prophecies that are inherent to that title. Jesus will literally reign on David's throne in Jerusalem during the Millennium and will continue to do so forevermore in the Eternal State.

GOD PROMISED A NEW COVENANT

During the Last Supper Jesus indicated that the New Covenant was to be instituted by the spilling of his blood for the forgiveness of sins (e.g., Matt 26:28). In speaking on the purpose of observing the ordinance of the Lord's Supper, Paul reminded the Gentile church in Corinth that Jesus had spoken of the New Covenant (1 Cor 11:25). Believers are made sufficient to be ministers of this covenant (2 Cor 3:6). The Epistle to the Hebrews provides extensive treatment on the New Covenant, indicating its active status (Heb 7:22; 8:6–13; 9:15; 10:16, 29; 12:24; 13:20). The New Covenant has been inaugurated and the Body of Christ currently enjoys some of its blessings. However, to then conclude that the New Covenant has met all of its objectives would be a hasty generalization. Covenants are devices that work themselves out over time as they mature.[10] The New Covenant is still engaged in this process.

The New Covenant was specifically promised to Israel. Jeremiah 31:31–34:

> Behold, the days are coming declares the LORD, when I will make
> a new covenant with the house of Israel and the house of Judah, not
> like the covenant that I made with their fathers on the day when I

---

10. A reasonable position given that the Abrahamic Covenant is still working toward the objective of placing the Jews in control of all of the Promised Land (Gen 15:18–21). The Mosaic Covenant had to work itself out for approximately 1,450 years before being fulfilled in Jesus (Matt 5:17).

took them by the hand to bring them out of the land of Egypt, my covenant that they broke, though I was their husband, declares the LORD. For this is the covenant that I will make with the house of Israel after those days, declares the LORD: I will put my law within them, and I will write it on their hearts. And I will be their God, and they shall be my people. And no longer shall each one teach his neighbor and each his brother, saying 'Know the LORD,' for they shall all know me, from the least of them to the greatest, declares the LORD. For I will forgive their iniquity, and I will remember their sin no more."

The New Covenant will only be completed when the entire nation of Israel is an involved party (v. 31). This covenant is identified as being distinct from the Mosaic Covenant (v. 32). The New Covenant is, in part, different in that it is unconditional. It is defined by God writing his law on the hearts of those in the house of Israel (v. 33). The people of Israel will finally have a complete fellowship with God. There will be no need for the Jews to evangelize to one another as they will all know the LORD and he will no longer remember their sin (v. 34).

The Jewish People Ingathered

Jesus the Redeemer will return to Zion and bring salvation to the Jews through the New Covenant (Isa 59:20–21). That the completed work of the New Covenant leads directly into the Millennial Kingdom is deduced from the description of the glory of God coming upon Israel (Isa 60). For this to happen the Hebrews will need to be ingathered back into the Promised Land. The New Covenant is closely associated with the Jews prospering in their land as seen in Jeremiah 32. God promised to gather the Jews back into the Promised Land (v. 37). The LORD proclaimed that the Jews will be his people and that he will be their God (v. 38). God will give his people one heart and one way (v. 39). The LORD then reaffirmed that he will make an everlasting covenant with the Jews. He will not turn away from them and they will not turn away from him (v. 40). The ingathering of the Jews is an integral part of the biblical narrative regarding the fulfillment of the New Covenant. It would be unnatural to try and separate the two.

After once again affirming that he would make an everlasting covenant with the Jews, God said the following in Ezekiel 37:26–28:

I will make a covenant of peace with them. It shall be an everlasting covenant with them. And I will set them in their land and multiply them, and will set my sanctuary in their midst forevermore. My dwelling place shall be with them, and I will be their God, and they shall be my people. Then the nations will know that I am the LORD who sanctifies Israel, when my sanctuary is in their midst forevermore."

The New Covenant is described as one of peace made between God and the Jewish people. The fulfillment of which is accompanied by the promise of a new temple sanctuary to then be constructed (v. 26). The rest of the world will finally come to recognize the God of Israel when his dwelling place is in their midst (vv. 27–28). This will happen during the Millennium.

The nations coming to recognize Jesus is further evidenced by them being required to travel to Jerusalem and pay him tribute (e.g., Isa 18:7; Zech 14:16–19). Obviously these prophecies have yet to occur. They cannot occur during the Eternal State as no one would be forced to worship Jesus in a world filled with only believers. There is no temple in the Eternal State, save the Lamb (Rev 21:22). There, then, must be a period of time where God reigns on the earth from his temple that occurs before the Eternal State. This period is the Millennium and the New Covenant leads into it.

A PRESERVED PEOPLE

The continued survival of the Jewish people throughout history is due to the providence and fidelity of God in keeping his promises. If the Jews were to ever be extinguished then God's unconditional covenants could never come to fruition, for the covenants belong to the Israelites (Rom 9:4). Consider that today there are no Kenites, Amorites, Canaanites, Moabites, Hittites, Jebusites, or any of a number of other ancient peoples. They either became extinct or were assimilated into other peoples and cultures. In contrast, the Jewish people retained a genetic, cultural, and national identity. They exist as a nation in both ethnicity and in ownership of their land.

The LORD is so concerned with keeping his promises that he equated the permanence of the cycles of nature to the permanence of the Israelites as a nation (Jer 31:35–36). He further emphasized the point in Jeremiah 31:37:

Thus says the LORD: "If the heavens above can be measured, and the foundations of the earth below can be explored, then I will cast off all the offspring of Israel for all that they have done, declares the LORD."

The LORD made a *reductio ad absurdum* statement that illustrates just how untenable it would be for him to abandon Israel. This was his powerful way of teaching that he would never cast off Israel as a result of the things they have done. There is nothing the Jews could do that would result in God reneging on what he has promised. Jeremiah 31:35–37 provides assurance that the New Covenant will be fulfilled by the inclusion of Israel. This will coincide with the Second Coming of Jesus (cf. Rom 11:26–29). It is in the Millennium when the Jews will finally enjoy all that has been promised to them in their covenants with God. Gentile believers in the Messiah will also enjoy the millennial blessings (e.g., Isa 56:1–8), for they are wild olives who have been grafted into the tree (Rom 11:17).[11]

The prince-of-preachers Charles Spurgeon preached:

I think we do not attach sufficient importance to the restoration of the Jews. We do not think enough about it. But certainly, if there is anything promised in the Bible it is this. I imagine that you cannot read the Bible without seeing clearly that there is to be an actual restoration of the Children of Israel . . . For when the Jews are restored, the fullness of the Gentiles shall be gathered in; and as soon as they return, then Jesus will come upon Mount Zion with his ancients gloriously, and the halcyon days of the millennium shall then dawn; we shall then know every man to be a brother and a friend; Christ shall rule with universal sway.[12]

11. The olive tree represents the commonwealth of Israel (cf. Eph 2:11–12) with the Abrahamic Covenant as its root.

12. Spurgeon, *Sermons*, 136.

3

The Millennial Kingdom

THERE IS A SENSE in which God's kingdom has always been active. This is true when it is defined as God's eternal and sovereign rule over the universe (Ps 10:16; 29:10; 103:19; Dan 4:3, 34–35). There is another sense of the Kingdom of God, which is the focus here, that can only be fully realized when all of the unconditional covenants have met each of their objectives. The covenants are the primary means through which the kingdom is brought about. While the covenants have been completing their work, the kingdom has been attempted or offered in various ways. Mystery elements of the kingdom program are active and some of its power has broken through into our present world. This has caused a great deal of confusion in the church as to what exactly the kingdom even is. A brief survey, including what its future fulfillment is supposed to look like and a timeline of its various forms, is necessary to appreciate the kingdom's nature. This exercise reveals that the kingdom has always been intended as an earthly and visible reign of God among his people. It also helps us to understand the purpose of the Millennium as a demonstration of the kingdom to a universe of believers and unbelievers alike.

DANIEL INTERPRETS KINGDOM DREAMS

A Great Image

The clearest explanation of the coming Kingdom of God comes from the Book of Daniel, especially in chapters two and seven. In chapter two, Nebuchadnezzar, the king of Babylon, has a dream of a great and frightening image with a head of gold, a chest and arms of silver, a core and thighs of bronze, legs of iron, and feet made of a mixture of iron and clay (vv. 31–33). All of the components of the statue are broken into pieces when a stone, not cut by a human hand, struck the feet of iron and clay. The pieces of the statue were blown away and the stone became a great mountain that filled the entire earth (vv. 34–35). Daniel prophetically interpreted the dream, telling Nebuchadnezzar that he, and by extension Babylon, was represented by the head of gold (v. 38). After Babylon, a lesser silver-kingdom was to arise (v. 39), Medo-Persia. This would be followed by the bronze kingdom (v. 39) of the Greek empire, and the iron kingdom (v. 40) of Rome. The feet of iron and clay is said to be a divided kingdom, partly strong and partly brittle (vv. 41–42). The feet are made from something like Rome, or her remains, plus other peoples. The feet are not said to be a distinct kingdom, and so we could consider them to represent Rome 2.0. This reconstructed kingdom will have ten toes, symbolizing kings (vv. 42–43; cf. Dan 7:24; Rev 17:12).

This brings us to the key passage of the chapter. Daniel 2:44–45:

> And in the days of those kings the God of heaven will set up a kingdom that shall never be destroyed, nor shall the kingdom be left to another people. It shall break in pieces all these kingdoms and bring them to an end, and it shall stand forever, just as you saw that a stone was cut from a mountain by no human hand, and that it broke in pieces the iron, the bronze, the clay, the silver, and the gold. A great God has made known to the king what shall be after this. The dream is certain, and its interpretation sure."

This divulges everything we need to know about when God's kingdom can be established. It can only come about during the days when ten kings rule over the final iteration of man's dominion (v. 44). This is a yet future scenario. God's kingdom will destroy and then supplant the kingdom of man. The idea is one of immediate replacement, not one of an overlap for thousands of years. The picture is of a stone striking the final human kingdom, instantly reducing the image to pieces to be blown away like chaff, leaving no trace of them (v. 45; cf. Dan 2:35). The mountain that the stone was cut from likely represents God (cf. Deut 32:18). A stone was used several times to symbolize the Messiah Jesus (Ps 118:22; Isa 8:14; 28:16; Zech 3:9; Rom 9:33; 1 Pet 2:6–8). The stone here would, then, seem to represent God's kingdom and her King Messiah, just as the head of gold represented Babylon and her king (cf. v. 38). The stone growing into a mountain and filling the entire earth was used to picture the total dominance of God's kingdom (v. 35). This mountain may be connected to the great mountain of Jerusalem, from where the Messiah will reign (cf. Isa 2:2–4). Regardless, the kingdom it portrays will never be destroyed (v. 44), just as was promised in the Davidic Covenant (2 Sam 7:16).

Underscoring the replacement of man's kingdom with God's is how Daniel speaks of Nebuchadnezzar in verses 37–38:

> You, O king, the king of kings, to whom the God of heaven has given the kingdom, the power, and the might, and the glory, and into whose hand he has given, wherever they dwell, the children of man, the beasts of the field, and the birds of the heavens, making you rule over them all—you are the head of gold.

Nebuchadnezzar was once the most powerful man alive. He was not just a king but held authority over other kings (v. 37). The LORD personally called Nebuchadnezzar a king of kings (Ezek 26:7). He was given dominion over all the nations and animals in that part of the world (v. 38; cf. Jer 27:6–7, 14). In this respect, Nebuchadnezzar serves as a kingdom of man counterpart to Jesus' office in God's kingdom. Jesus will reign as the true King of kings (1 Tim 6:15; Rev 17:14; 19:16), over not just part of the earth, but all of it (Zech 14:9). God gave Nebuchadnezzar a kingdom, power, and glory (v. 37). In teaching on how to pray, Jesus included the fact that God has his own kingdom, power, and glory (Matt 6:13).[1] Nebuchadnezzar and Babylon were visible and earthly powers, just as the empires that followed. When the great image is destroyed and replaced with the great mountain, the Messiah and his kingdom will be all the more visible and earthly.

Four Beasts

A companion dream is found in Daniel 7 that both confirms the interpretation of Nebuchadnezzar's and provides us with more information and insight. This time the dream that Daniel interprets is his own, one envisioning four beasts that represent kings and their kingdoms (v. 17). Each one rose out of the sea that is the peoples of the world (vv. 2–3; cf. Rev 17:15). The first beast, representing Babylon, was a lion with eagle wings that were later plucked. Then, it was made to stand on two feet and given the mind of a man (v. 4). Nebuchadnezzar and Babylon were compared to a lion and

---

1. In some manuscripts, Matthew 6:13 ends with the clause: *For yours is the kingdom and the power and the glory, forever. Amen.*

an eagle in several other passages (e.g., Jer 4:7; Ezek 13:3). Nebuchadnezzar was greatly humbled, followed by his mind being returned to him (Dan 4:28–37). The second beast, representing Medo-Persia, was a devouring bear on its side with three ribs in its mouth (v. 5). The Persians defeated the three considerable powers of Lydia, Babylon, and Egypt. The third beast, representing the Greek Empire, was a four-headed leopard with four bird-like wings (v. 6). After Alexander the Great died, the empire was divided among his four generals in Asia Minor, Egypt, Macedonia, and Syria (cf. Dan 8:8). The first three kingdoms came to pass, matching their detailed descriptions. The same, then, should be expected from the forth.

The forth beast had iron teeth; it was terrifying and extraordinarily strong. This beast represents Rome, extending into her latter form of being mixed with other peoples (cf. Dan 2:41–43). The remainder of the previous kingdoms were devoured, crushed, and trampled. This final beast has ten horns and is specifically said to be different from all those before (v. 7; Rev 13:1), and that it will conquer the entire earth (v. 23). The ten horns are ten kings that will arise out of this final kingdom (Rev 17:12). One of them is distinct from the others and will subdue three of them (vv. 8, 24). This horn has the eyes of a man and a mouth that is used to utter boasts and to speak against the Most High God (vv. 8, 25). This evil king will wear down the saints and attempt to alter to the times and the law.[2] Control over both will be handed over to him for a period of three and one-half years (v. 25).[3] This wicked ruler is referred to as the man of lawlessness by Paul (2 Thess 2:3–9), and the coming Antichrist and the beast rising from the abyss by John (1 John 2:18; Rev 11:7). In directly referencing Daniel, Jesus warned of the abomination of desolation that the Antichrist will bring (Matt 24:15; cf. Dan 9:27; 12:11; 2 Thess 2:4). The Messiah further warned of a great tribulation, a time worse than any other in history, that will then take place (Matt 24:21; cf. Jer 30:7). The Antichrist is the personification and head over man's kingdom going to sinful extremes in its twilight.

He and his dominion will be annihilated and taken away forever (v. 26). It is at this time that the sovereignty of all of man's kingdoms under the heavens will be transferred to the people of the saints of the Most High for them to possess forever (vv. 18, 27; cf. Rev 11:15). It is explicitly written that their reign will be upon the earth (Rev 5:10). This could hardly be understood as being fulfilled at present. The saints are not reigning over the

---

2. *Times* may refer to the feasts and Sabbaths or the calendar.

3. The meaning of *time, times, and half a time* (cf. Dan 4:16; Rev 11:2–3; 12:6; 13:15).

world when they are being beheaded, tortured, mocked, and minimalized by the world. Once begun, the Kingdom of God will be everlasting, with all the power structures on earth serving him (v. 27). Though the dominion of the kingdoms of man will be taken away, their peoples will still be permitted to survive for a season (v. 12; cf. Zech 14:16). This informs us that once the Kingdom of God begins there will be a period of time where those who do not fully trust in the Messiah will still be living on the earth. Therefore, there must be an intermediary period between the end of the kingdoms of man and the beginning of the sin-free Eternal State. The Millennium is that intermediary age.

The Son of Man is Given a Kingdom

Daniel further wrote on how the Messiah will come to take charge of his kingdom in verses 13–14:

> *"I saw in the night visions, and behold, with the clouds of heaven there came one like a son of man, and he came to the Ancient of Days and was presented before him. And to him was given dominion and glory and a kingdom, that all peoples, nations, and languages should serve him; his dominion is an everlasting dominion, which shall not pass away, and his kingdom one that shall not be destroyed.*

Simply understood is that when the Son of Man, the Messiah, comes upon the clouds, it is at that time when he will be given dominion and a kingdom (v. 13). The kingdom is marked by all peoples on earth having to serve the Messiah (v. 14), something that most certainly is not happening in the present age. Jesus referenced this passage as a sign of his return, that when after a time of tribulation, all the peoples of the earth will see him coming on the clouds (Matt 24:29–30). The apostle John alluded to this passage, teaching that when Jesus comes on the clouds every eye will see him and that all of the peoples of the earth will mourn over him (Rev 1:7; cf. Zech 12:10). Therefore, the Messiah and his apostle both place the inauguration of the kingdom, as envisioned by Daniel, at the Second Coming. It will be an astonishing and unmistakable event that no one on earth will miss. All of the intricate details of Daniel's interpretations, and the precise timeline he provides, must be fulfilled before the Kingdom of God replaces the final kingdom of man. It is then when the power of world-wide governance will be handed over to the Messiah and his saints (cf. Obad 1:21). Man's rule will end and the Messiah's will begin.

KINGDOM AT CREATION

Narratives on the Kingdom of God literally bookend the Bible. The kingdom's loss and expectation of its restoration is the very saga of the Scriptures. This is the theme of the Bible and the overall story it tells. The kingdom was active in the Garden of Eden with God and Adam and Eve. We can reasonably infer that God sought fellowship with Adam and Eve regularly. It is unlikely that the first time he walked through the Garden to visit was when the couple were hiding in shame (Gen 3:18). Earth was God's chosen place of communing with his people. This represents the purest form of the kingdom, a time and place where there is no sin and God's people fellowship with him.

Because Adam sinned, he and Eve were exiled from the Garden to work the ground for their food and to eventually die (Gen 3:17–23). Their exit marked the end of the kingdom, for man was now separated from God by an immeasurable gulf. The LORD was so concerned that Adam and Eve may be able to get back in and eat from the Tree of Life, and thus live forever, that he placed cherubim and a flaming sword to guard the east entrance (Gen 3:22, 24). Man having access to the Tree of Life is connected to God's kingdom being in operation. This is why similar trees are present in the Millennium (Ezek 47:12; cf. Isa 65:22), and why the Tree of Life grows in the Eternal State (Rev 22:2, 14).

In conjunction with making man in the image of God, he made humans to rule over all the animals of the sea, earth, and sky. Adam and Eve were ordered to be fruitful and multiply so that the earth would be subdued (Gen 1:26–28). Though the kingdom ended with Adam and Eve's banishment from the Garden, a good portion of humanity's dominion over the earth remained. Psalm 8 confirms this in teaching that man is only a little lower than the heavenly beings, crowned with glory and honor (v. 5). God gave men dominion over the works of his hands and put all things under their feet (v. 6), including beasts, birds, and sea life (vv. 7–8). Remember that this is the position that Nebuchadnezzar, as the representative over man's kingdom, is described as having. The kingdoms of man as described in Daniel 2 and 7 are that of men ruling according to their own desires. Man retained much of his dominion, but his management of it was misdirected away from serving God. The course is corrected with the saints reigning under the Messiah at the commencement of God's kingdom.

After the fall of man there was no kingdom. During this period God governed the world primarily through intervention. When the LORD saw that the wickedness of man was great on the earth he sent the flood (Gen 6–7). When people came together from the east in a plain in Shinar to build a tower and glorify themselves the LORD came down and confused their language, dispersing them over the face of the earth (Gen 11:1–9). God would at times speak to individuals and even visit with them, as he did with Abraham (e.g., Gen 18). But these occasions were always brief.

A KINGDOM OF PRIESTS

Though promises were made to Abraham and his descendants through Jacob, the Israelites were not part of a kingdom for over four centuries. After the Exodus from Egypt the people came to Mount Sinai. It was there where the LORD instructed Moses to tell the house of Jacob the following in Exodus 19:4–6:

> You yourselves have seen what I did to the Egyptians, and how I bore you on eagles' wings and brought you to myself. Now therefore, if you will indeed obey my voice and keep my covenant, you shall be my treasured possession among all peoples, for all the earth is mine; and you shall be to me a kingdom of priests and a holy nation. These are the words that you shall speak to the people of Israel."

Finally, God once again looked to establish a kingdom! Here is the first reference in Scripture to a kingdom unto God. Israel was about to become a kingdom of priests, meaning that each citizen would have access to God. This would also make her a holy nation in that she was to be separated from the others, entering into a special relationship with the LORD (v. 6). The covenant was entered into by the people when they agreed to obey all that the LORD had spoken (Exod 19:8). This meant that they would have to obey God's voice and keep his covenant (v. 5).

A ceremony to ratify the covenant is recorded in Exodus 24:6–8. Moses took blood from young bulls and sprinkled it on the basins and the altar (v. 6). After he read from the book of the covenant before the people, they affirmed that they would be obedient to all that the LORD had spoken (v. 7). In response, Moses took some of the blood and sprinkled it on the Israelites, proclaiming that it confirmed the covenant made in accordance with all of the LORD's instructions (v. 8). The birth of Israel as both a nation and a kingdom is intertwined with the inauguration of the Mosaic Covenant (Exod 19–24). Israel remaining a kingdom unto God depended upon the people staying in a covenant relationship with him.

During this time of beginnings the LORD made a special appearance, coming down upon the mountain in the form of fire (Exod 19:18; 24:16–17). God determined that the Israelites would hear him speaking to Moses (Exod 19:9). This let the people know that their Creator had chosen Moses to have authority over them. They could never doubt that it was God's law that Moses was enforcing. Further governmental hierarchy can be gleaned from Exodus 24. Moses, Aaron, his oldest sons Nadab and Abihu, and seventy of the elders of Israel traveled part way up the mountain (vv. 1, 9, 14). There, they were blessed to see God on what appeared to be a platform of sapphire (v. 10). Despite seeing the LORD, the elders of Israel remained unharmed, enjoying fellowship as they ate and drink (v. 11). Moses alone went further up the mountain to receive the stone tablets of the law (vv. 2, 12–13). He ordered the elders to stay where they were (v. 14). The glory of the LORD rested on Mount Sinai, speaking to Moses for forty days and forty nights (vv. 16, 18). This glory is the dwelling or nesting presence of the LORD, also known as the *Shekinah*. The people of Israel could see the Shekinah glory from afar, as a consuming fire (v. 17). The proximity that one had in relation to the LORD revealed his or her place in the kingdom. The structure of rule began with God as the supreme authority, then Moses, then the elders, and finally the Israelites in general. This was the theocratic kingdom of Israel in her infancy. Being great in the kingdom yields the reward of being closer to God. This principle is highly applicable to life in the Millennium.

Squandered Potential

On Exodus 19:5–6, Thomas Constable noted:

> In short, Israel could have become a testimony to the whole world, of how glorious it can be to live under the government of God. The people experienced these blessings only partially, because their obedience was partial. Israel's disobedience to the Mosaic Covenant did not invalidate any of God's promises to Abraham, however. Those promises did not rest on Israel's obedience, as these did (cf. Gen. 15:17–21 and Exod. 19:5–6).[4]

Israel's kingdom power matched the level to which she stayed obedient to the LORD. Surely God's desire was for the nation to show complete fidelity

---

4. Constable, *Notes on Exodus*, 115.

toward him. As such, the kingdom of Israel not only had the potential to overwhelm the world, but this was God's ideal for her.

God's aspiration for Israel's exaltation is clearly expressed in Deuteronomy 28:1 and 28:13:

> *And if you faithfully obey the voice of the LORD your God, being careful to do all his commandments that I command you today, the LORD your God will set you high above all the nations of the earth.*

> *And the LORD will make you the head and not the tail, and you shall only go up and not down, if you obey the commandments of the LORD your God, which I command you today, being careful to do them,*

Because Israel could not obey perfectly, she never extended the power of the Kingdom of God over the nations of the earth. However, God was not thwarted and his plan cannot be resisted. In the coming kingdom, people from mighty nations will flow to Jerusalem to entreat the favor of the LORD and learn his ways (Isa 2:2–4; Mic 4:1–3; Zech 8:22–23). Finally, God's purpose for Israel as head of the nations within the Kingdom of God will be realized. The nations, with many not knowing God, will witness his kingdom.

The Kingdom Divided

As Israel became more degenerate, the kingdom decayed until it finally ceased. Even from the time of Jacob, the twelve tribes of Israel quarreled with each other (Gen 37:3–11). The disunity continued through the government of the judges, with the most notable conflict being a civil war against the sons of Benjamin. After another war against the rebelling Benjamites (2 Sam 2–3), David finally united the tribes, becoming king over all of Israel (2 Sam 5:1–3). The consensus did not last long as David's own son Absalom declared himself to be the new king, drawing away some of the people's loyalty (2 Sam 15:10–12). More Israelites withdrew from David, when Sheba, noted to be a worthless fellow, led an insurrection (2 Sam 20:1–2).

Increased strife came under the reign of King Solomon when Jeroboam rose up against him. Jeroboam was encouraged to seek power upon hearing the prophecy of Ahijah the Shilonite. God told the prophet Ahijah, that because of the Israel's sin under the king's leadership, he would tear ten of the tribes from Solomon's son and hand them over to Jeroboam (1 Kgs

11:26–38). Solomon's family was guaranteed to maintain control over one tribe so that David would always have a line of kings before the LORD in Jerusalem, the city where he determined to put his name (1 Kgs 11:32, 34, 36). Only by the power of God's faithfulness to the Davidic Covenant did Solomon remain a king (cf. Ps 89). The LORD said that he would afflict the children of David over their disobedience, but also that it would not last forever (1 Kgs 11:39).

Rehoboam succeeded his father Solomon in becoming the next king. When he denied Jeroboam and the people's request for a lower tax rate, ten of the tribes rejected the house of David (1 Kgs 12:12–16). The ten tribes chose Jeroboam as their new king, leaving only Judah to David's family (1 Kgs 12:20). Thus, the prophecy of Ahijah was fulfilled (1 Kgs 12:15). Later, the tribe of Benjamin allied with Judah in an effort to bring reprisal upon the rebels. However, Rehoboam heeded the words of the LORD, as spoken through the prophet Shemaiah, and turned back (1 Kgs 12:21–24). Benjamin remained joined to Judah.

The LORD gave Jeroboam the opportunity to serve him and lead a moral kingdom (1 Kgs 11:38). Instead, Jeroboam brought more contrast with Judah by making two golden calves, one in Bethel and one in Dan, for his people to worship. The idea behind them being that the people would no longer need to travel to the temple in Jerusalem to offer sacrifices. This would prevent them from becoming convicted and turning back to the LORD (1 Kgs 12:26–30). Jeroboam further consolidated his kingdom by building temples on high places and instituting a fraudulent Feast of Tabernacles that was celebrated a month late (1 Kgs 12:31–33). The Feast of Tabernacles represents the Kingdom of God in that the people dwell with their Creator. Fittingly, the corrupt feast in Israel under Jeroboam represented the new pagan kingdom. The kingdom was now truly divided, with the depraved kingdom of Israel or Ephraim in the north and the more legitimate kingdom of Judah in the south.

The kingdom in the north became ever the more sinful by following foreign customs, serving idols, sacrificing their children, and rejecting the LORD's commandments and his Covenant (2 Kgs 17:8–22). In 721 BC, the northern kingdom was carried away into exile in Assyria as punishment (2 Kgs 17:23). Meanwhile, the southern kingdom of Judah was ruled by King Hezekiah; he did right in the sight of the LORD (2 Kgs 18:3). After his death it did not take long for Judah to play the whore just as Israel did (cf. Jer 3:8). From 606–587 BC, Babylon besieged Judah, her people were taken captive through three deportations, and the temple and Jerusalem were desolated (2 Kgs 24–25).

It is the LORD's purpose for the kingdom in Israel that she be united and holy unto him. He has promised to bring this to pass in several passages, including Isaiah 11:12–13:

> He will raise a signal for the nations and will assemble the banished of Israel, and gather the dispersed of Judah from the four corners of the earth. The jealousy of Ephraim shall depart, and those who harass Judah shall be cut off; Ephraim shall not be jealous of Judah, and Judah shall not harass Ephraim.

Sin brings division to any kingdom. Thankfully, the Messiah can overcome the sins of men, bringing unity. When Jesus reigns from Israel during the Millennial Kingdom, the tribes will truly serve their God and no division among them will remain.

The Kingdom Departed

From the moment of Israel's birth at Sinai the Shekinah stayed with her. The glory of the LORD dwelled among his people in the holy of holies, often between the two cherubim on top of the ark of the covenant, first in the Tabernacle and then in Solomon's temple. Finally, the dwelling presence of the LORD could tolerate no more sin and departed from the people in Ezekiel 10:18–19 and 11:22–23:

> Then the glory of the LORD went out from the threshold of the house, and stood over the cherubim. And the cherubim lifted up their wings and mounted up from the earth before my eyes as they went out, with the wheels beside them. And they stood at the entrance of the east gate of the house of the LORD, and the glory of the God of Israel was over them.

> Then the cherubim lifted up their wings, with the wheels beside them, and the glory of the God of Israel was over them. And the glory of the LORD went up from the midst of the city and stood on the mountain that is on the east side of the city.

The Shekinah was so reluctant to leave that the LORD's presence remained over the threshold for a time. It did the same over the east gate, the city, and finally on the Mount of Olives before completing its departure. Compare this to the immediacy of the Shekinah rushing into the Tabernacle (Exod 40:34–35), Solomon's temple (1 Kgs 8:10–11), and when it returns to the millennial temple (Ezek 43:1–5). God is quick to be with his people and slow to depart. The Shekinah glory's departure marked the end of the kingdom. There can be no Kingdom of God without God.

THE GOSPEL OF THE KINGDOM

The theme of Matthew's Gospel is Jesus Christ as King and the Kingdom of God. Matthew wrote of the offer of the King and the kingdom he brings, mysteries and parables about the kingdom, and Israel's rejection of the King and thus the kingdom. The Jews were expecting a literal, earthly, and Davidic kingdom, fulfilling the covenant promises and the words of the prophets. No new definition of the kingdom is ever given. If the kingdom now suddenly meant something else, then surely the apostles or Jesus would have indicated so.

We begin with John the Baptist and his core message as it is summed up in Matthew 3:2:

> "Repent, for the kingdom of heaven is at hand."

While the other Gospel writers used the name *Kingdom of God*, Matthew usually preferred to use the synonym, *Kingdom of Heaven*. The Greek *eggizo* (eng-id'-zo) translated above as *at hand*, means to bring near or to approach (cf. Matt 2:1). Thus, the kingdom was said to be *near* not *here*. This may come off as obvious, and yet the mistake of conflating the two is often made, resulting in significant interpretive errors. Many Jews believed that they would inherit the kingdom in virtue of having Abraham as their father (Matt 3:9). But if the people were to receive the kingdom they had to repent, turning from their sins in anticipation of the Messiah. After John the Baptist was arrested, Jesus took over preaching the same message (Matt 4:17).

With the context in mind, consider the Lord's Prayer anew. Jesus provided it as a model for how his disciples were to pray (cf. Luke 11:1–4). Every petition in the prayer relates to the kingdom, with the first three concerning its coming. Matthew 6:9–10:

> Pray then like this: "Our Father in heaven, hallowed be your name. Your kingdom come, your will be done, on earth as it is in heaven.

The reverence for God's name and the kingdom in Israel are directly linked. When the Israelites were scattered among the nations, it profaned God's name (Ezek 36:19–21). This is why the second petition of the prayer is for the kingdom to come. The LORD's name will be fully vindicated before the nations when the Jews are back in the Promised Land, partaking in the New Covenant, and enjoying a personal relationship with him (Isa 29:22–23; Ezek 36:22–38). The kingdom will be manifested on the earth, just as it is currently so in heaven.

William James Durant, the eminent 20th century historian, came to the same conclusion:

> What did he mean by the Kingdom? A supernatural heaven? Apparently not, for the apostles and the early Christians unanimously expected an earthly Kingdom. This was the Jewish tradition that Christ inherited; and he taught his followers to pray to the Father, "Thy Kingdom come, thy will be done on earth as it is in heaven . . ."[5]

The Messiah commissioned the apostles to preach the gospel of the kingdom in Matthew 10:5–7:

> These twelve Jesus sent out, instructing them, "Go nowhere among the Gentiles and enter no town of the Samaritans, but go rather to the lost sheep of the house of Israel. And proclaim as you go, saying, 'The kingdom of heaven is at hand.'

The apostles were ordered to limit their ministry to the Jews only. They could not preach on the kingdom to the Gentiles or even to the Samaritans, who had some Jewish blood. Even though people from every nation would be able to enjoy the kingdom, its coming was solely dependent upon Israel's response.

As Jesus and his apostles preached, the message started to be rejected. Jesus changed his tenor in response, denouncing those cities where his miracles had been done but yet not responded to with repentance (Matt 11:20–24). The Pharisees made things irreparable, when as leaders of Israel, they attributed the Spirit's work through Jesus to Satan (Matt 12:22–24). Such blasphemy against the Spirit was so severe that Jesus said it could not be forgiven, either in the current age or the one to come (Matt 12:31–32).

---

5. Durant, *Caesar and Christ*, 564–565.

The Kingdom's Mystery Age

In transitioning to chapter 13, Matthew-scholar Stanley Toussaint commented:

> *The die is cast. The religious leaders have openly declared their oppo-*
> *sition to their Messiah. The people of Israel are amazed at the power*
> *of Jesus and His speech, but they fail to recognize Him as their King.*
> *Not seeing the Messiahship of Jesus in His words and works, they*
> *have separated the fruit from the tree. Because of this opposition*
> *and spiritual apathy, the King adapts His teaching method and the*
> *doctrine concerning the coming of the kingdom to the situation.*[6]

Matthew 13 opens with the words *that same day*, connecting it to Jesus'
rejection via the unpardonable sin in the previous chapter (v. 1). Jesus now
began to work from the position that he had been rejected as King Messiah. This rejection would only grow until it culminated in him going to the
cross. Consequently, the kingdom was no longer available to Israel at this
time. No longer would Jesus preach on the nearness of the kingdom. He
still continued to teach on the kingdom, but readjusted the focus toward
its mysteries.

Matthew 13:10–11:

> *Then the disciples came and said to him, "Why do you speak to them*
> *in parables?" And he answered them, "To you it has been given to*
> *know the secrets of the kingdom of heaven, but to them it has not*
> *been given.*

These newly presented teachings on the kingdom were secrets or mysteries,
meaning that they were never clearly disclosed to any of the prophets (cf.
Col 1:26). A previously unknown period in the overall prophetic program
of the kingdom was being revealed (cf. Eph 3:4–6). This is the current age,
one between the First and Second Coming. The fact that this period was
hidden from the prophets is precisely why their teachings on the two com-
ings of Jesus are intertwined. The parables were for the concealing of the
truth from the unbelieving multitudes and for the revealing of the truth to
those few who did believe (v. 11).

The parable of the sower is on the gospel of the kingdom (vv. 3–8;
18–23). Those who heard and understood were empowered to bear fruit (v.
23). The next six parables were for the purpose of teaching on this mystery
age as it relates to the kingdom's future fulfillment. In this new era, the

---

6. Toussaint, *Behold the King*, 156.

tares, representing the sons of the Devil, would grow among the wheat, representing the sons of the kingdom. Only when this age ends will the tares be separated from the wheat, to be gathered and burned (vv. 24–30; 36–43). Both those who truly know Jesus and those who merely say they do are grouped together, just as a dragnet catches good and bad fish. Angels will remove the wicked from among the righteous and throw them into the furnace (vv. 47–50). Sin, typified by leaven (cf. Exod 12:15; Matt 16:6; 1 Cor 5:6–9), will continue to increase in the interim (v. 33).

Big things have small beginnings. The mustard seed, small like Jesus' ministry, would ultimately bring forth the long awaited Kingdom of God (vv. 31–32). The kingdom had been hidden for hundreds of years, ever since the Shekinah departed the temple. Those Jews now blessed enough to stumble upon this treasure should be willing to sacrifice everything for it (v. 44). Likewise, the Jews who were actively looking for the kingdom and found it should have been eager to sell all they had for this pearl of great price (vv. 45–46). No amount of wealth, possessions, or attachments could ever match the value of inheriting the kingdom.

Jesus later alluded to the current age in Matthew 22:41–45:

> Now while the Pharisees were gathered together, Jesus asked them a question, saying, "What do you think about the Christ? Whose son is he?" They said to him, "The son of David." He said to them, "How is it then that David, in the Spirit, calls him Lord, saying, "'The Lord said to my Lord, "Sit at my right hand, until I put your enemies under your feet"'"? If then David calls him Lord, how is he his son?"

In quoting Psalm 110:1, Jesus proved from Scripture that the Messiah was both the descendant of David and his divine Lord. This verse also prophecies the very timetable of the kingdom that the New Testament reveals. After his rejection, Jesus ascended to the Father to sit at his right hand (cf. Acts 2:33; Heb 1:3; Rev 3:21; 12:5). During this period the enemies of Jesus are permitted to continue (cf. Isa 42:3; Matt 12:20). Their rebellion will end with the Messiah returning to the earth to inaugurate the kingdom (cf. Rev 19:15).

The Kingdom Postponed

With his rejection as the Davidic King firmly established, Jesus severely chastised the scribes and the Pharisees for almost the entirety of Matthew

23. At the same time, he lamented over the people of Jerusalem, saying the following in verses 37–39:

> "O Jerusalem, Jerusalem, the city that kills the prophets and stones those who are sent to it! How often would I have gathered your children together as a hen gathers her brood under her wings, and you were not willing! See, your house is left to you desolate. For I tell you, you will not see me again, until you say, 'Blessed is he who comes in the name of the Lord.'"

What a yearning desire Jesus had to shelter his people! Jerusalem's *house* seems to refer to the temple, the Davidic Dynasty, and the people as a whole. The nation was to become hollow, absent the Messiah, until the people finally attributed the Messianic blessing to Jesus (v. 39; cf. Ps 118:26; Hos 5:15; Zech 12:10).

The kingdom's postponement is made most obvious in Matthew 25:31–34:

> "When the Son of Man comes in his glory, and all the angels with him, then he will sit on his glorious throne. Before him will be gathered all the nations, and he will separate people one from another as a shepherd separates the sheep from the goats. And he will place the sheep on his right, but the goats on the left. Then the King will say to those on his right, 'Come, you who are blessed by my Father, inherit the kingdom prepared for you from the foundation of the world.

Jesus was quite clear in saying that he will sit on his throne when he comes again. This unmistakable event has the Messiah coming in full glory and surrounded by angels. He will separate the saved from the unsaved, bringing those who love him into the then established kingdom. Nothing like this happened at Pentecost, in 70 AD with the destruction of Jerusalem, or at any other point in history thus far. Put simply, the kingdom will only begin when Jesus returns to make it happen. You cannot have a kingdom without a king.

STILL COMING

The conclusion that the kingdom did not come in the gospel accounts is vindicated with the apostles' question and Jesus' response in Acts 1:6–7:

> So when they had come together, they asked him, "Lord, will you at this time restore the kingdom to Israel?" He said to them, "It is not

for you to know times or seasons that the Father has fixed by his own authority.

The apostles had just finished a forty day intensive where Jesus himself taught on the kingdom of God (Acts 1:3). Upon completing the course, the eleven understood that the kingdom would be restored to Israel. This is the context from which the question arose. If the kingdom had already returned or been established, even in some sense, then surely the Lord would have denounced the question. Instead, Jesus verified it as legitimate in answering that the timing of the kingdom's return was not for the apostles to know. In other words, the kingdom will be restored to Israel at some point according to the Father's timetable.

The kingdom surely did not arrive with Pentecost in Acts 2, given that it was still something expected by Peter in Acts 3:17–21. He preached to his countrymen that Jesus had fulfilled the prophecies concerning the Messiah's suffering (vv. 17–18). Peter then implored the men of Israel to change their minds regarding Jesus so that they may experience the anticipated times of refreshing (vv. 19–20). This time will commence with the Second Coming of Christ Jesus (v. 20). Only then will the restoration of all the things spoken of by the prophets come to pass (v. 21). This would certainly include the promises made by God concerning the return of the Jews to the Promised Land and the blessings to be experienced therein (e.g., Isa 11:11; Ezek 36:24; Amos 9:13–15), with Jesus as their King reigning from Jerusalem (e.g., Isa 24:23; Zech 14:17). The coming of the kingdom, then, remained contingent upon the nation of Israel trusting in Jesus as the Messiah.

The Jewish elders and the Pharisees arrested the deacon Stephen and brought him before the Sanhedrin, the ruling council of Israel (Acts 6:12). Stephen then witnessed to the high priest and the rest of Israel's leaders, referring to them as brothers and fathers (Acts 7:1–53). Upon completion of his speech, Stephen gazed into heaven and saw Jesus standing at the right hand of God (Acts 7:55). This is unique among the descriptions of Jesus being at the right hand of God; the others picture him sitting. Stephen even made it a point to proclaim the vision to his audience (Acts 7:56). Perhaps Jesus was standing to welcome Stephen home as the first Christian martyr (Acts 7:57–60). It is also entirely possible that as Stephen witnessed to the rulers of Israel, Jesus tentatively stood up in anticipation of them being moved by the deacon's words. For if Israel had believed on Jesus as a result of the speech, the Messiah would have returned.

Two Coming Kingdoms

Paul's discourse on the resurrection of the dead provides us with an important kingdom distinction in 1 Corinthians 15:23–25:

> *But each in his own order: Christ the firstfruits, then at his coming those who belong to Christ. Then comes the end, when he delivers the kingdom to God the Father after destroying every rule and every authority and power. For he must reign until he has put all his enemies under his feet.*

The Messiah must reign over his kingdom until he has defeated all of his enemies. Once this is accomplished, Jesus will hand over the kingdom to the Father. This speaks to the transitional nature of the Millennium. Unbelievers will continue on for the duration and stage one final rebellion before being permanently defeated (Rev 20:7–9). The Son's kingdom is the Millennium and the Father's Kingdom is the Eternal State. Each has his own kingdom and they should not be confused or conflated.

On the millennial implications of the passage, D. Edmond Hiebert wrote:

> *it is not only possible but probable that Paul understood this final triumph to take place during the millennial reign of Christ. To sum up the principal evidence, Paul's use of epeita ('after that') and eita ('then') in 1 Corinthians 15:23–24, the syntax of 15:24–25, and the parallel use of Psalms 8 and 110 in 1 Corinthians 15 and Hebrews 1 and 2 all point to the understanding that when Paul mentioned a kingdom and reign in 15:24–25, he referred to the reign of Christ on this earth following His return and prior to the eternal state, a time that Revelation 20:4–6 calls 'the thousand years.'*[7]

A Future Earthly Kingdom

The apostle John finally witnessed the coming of the kingdom as recorded in Revelation. One of the most critical kingdom verses is 5:10:

> *and you have made them a kingdom and priests to our God, and they shall reign on the earth."*

Those who have been ransomed by the blood of Jesus (Rev 5:9) have become positional members of the kingdom. Regarding when their actual

---

7. Hiebert, "Evidence from 1 Corinthians 15," 234.

reign begins, the future tense is used. The reign itself is specifically said to be on the earth. In no way did John see a current kingdom reign that was limited to a heavenly realm. The saints will receive authority to rule over the nations from Jesus, just as he received authority from the Father. Not only will Jesus rule with a rod of iron (e.g., Rev 12:5; 19:15), but so too will the saints (Rev 2:26–27). Critics of Premillennialism commonly argue that Revelation 20:1–6 never teaches that the saints will rule on earth. However, the clarity of Revelation 5:10 absolutely quashes this line of attack. Rest assured, when the saints are raised at the beginning of the Millennium as priests of God and Christ, they will rule with him for a thousand years (Rev 20:6), on this very world. A future terrestrial rule of saints under the Messiah is just the definition of the Kingdom of God that Daniel prophesied (Dan 7:27).

Following the Millennium, heaven and earth will be replaced with a new heaven and a new earth. The New Jerusalem will descend, resulting in man and God sharing the same home (Rev 21:1–2). This is a return to the intimate relationship people had with their Creator in Eden. There will no longer be death, crying or pain, for the world where those things happened will have passed away (Rev 21:4). From his throne, God will proclaim that he is making all things new, followed with the declaration, *it is done!* (Rev 21:6). Creation itself will be fully redeemed (cf. Rom 8:19–22). This is the final and perfect form of the kingdom, one that will last for eternity.

NOT YET

There is a popular theory on the Kingdom of God, first developed in the early 20th century by Geerhardus Vos, known as, *already but not yet*. The notion holds that the saints are currently partaking in the kingdom, while at the same time awaiting its arrival in a fuller and more glorious expression. There are many premillennialists who espouse such a view in one form or another. However, for the sake of biblical clarity, the sense of the kingdom which fulfills the unconditional covenants, chiefly the Davidic King ruling on earth, is yet to come. Whatever position one takes, an emphasis on the *not yet* is critical in understanding the story of the Scriptures.

"Problem" Passages

There are a few passages which are wrongly used to teach that the kingdom has already come. Two of which are frequently summoned. The first is Matthew 12:27–28:

> And if I cast out demons by Beelzebul, by whom do your sons cast them out? Therefore they will be your judges. But if it is by the Spirit of God that I cast out demons, then the kingdom of God has come upon you.

Remember that Jesus was responding to the unpardonable sin that the Pharisees had just committed in attributing his works to Satan (Matt 12:24, 32). The kingdom had come *upon* them, meaning that it was right next to them with the presence of the King. It could hardly mean that the Pharisees were entering the kingdom, for Jesus soon after assured them that they will not be forgiven in the age to come (Matt 12:32).

The second passage is the related Luke 17:20–21:

> Being asked by the Pharisees when the kingdom of God would come, he answered them, "The kingdom of God is not coming in ways that can be observed, nor will they say, 'Look, here it is!' or 'There!' for behold, the kingdom of God is in the midst of you."

Some translations read, *the kingdom of God is within you*. Such a rendering does not represent the Greek clearly in modern English. *In the midst of you,* is accurate and so none should think that the kingdom is literally inside people. The Pharisees' question may have been in response to Jesus' recent teaching that the kingdom had been postponed (cf. Luke 13:31–35). Even in answering that the kingdom was in the midst of the Pharisees, in the form of King Jesus, he still spoke of it as something yet to come. No one will be able to observe the coming of the kingdom incrementally over an extended period. For when the kingdom does come, it will do so suddenly. Declarations that the kingdom has come or that it is somewhere else will be unnecessary. The inauguration of the kingdom will be a super obvious, world-wide event. The coming of the Son of Man will be as lightning from the east that instantaneously shines as far as the west (Matt 24:27). Luke 17:20–21 verifies Daniel's prophecy of the immediacy with which the Kingdom of God arrives (Dan 2:34–35, 44).

Some passages which generically teach about a kingdom can cause confusion, such as Colossians 1:13. The point here is of a legal transfer of the believer from the domain of darkness to the kingdom of God's Son. The teaching was not aimed at establishing an already inaugurated kingdom. Ephesians, Colossians' sister epistle, clarifies this matter further. Believers are seated with Jesus in the heavenly places of Christ (Eph 2:6). This is where the saint's citizenship resides even if he or she is not physically present there. An American citizen would remain as such while he or she sojourned in another country for a season. Members of the Body are ambassadors for Christ (2 Cor 5:20), representing his kingdom, which is not of this world (John 18:36).

Still other verses can cause confusion because their context is overlooked; such is the case with Revelation 1:6. This verse too speaks of a positional place in the coming kingdom. Revelation 5:10 also teaches that the saints have been made into a kingdom of priests unto God, adding that they will reign upon the earth. The time of rule within the kingdom is still future. Passages that are unclear on a subject should be governed by those passages that speak directly to the topic. This basic rule of hermeneutics is especially true when applied to the Kingdom of God. The few murky passages are easily understood in light of the clear ones. And there are many more, not covered here, that speak of the kingdom as something still to come (e.g., 1 Cor 6:9; Gal 5:21; Eph 5:5).

Upon a consistent and contextual reading of the pertinent passages, it becomes readily apparent that Lewis Sperry Chafer was correct in writing: *Judging from the mass of Christian writings and from utterances in public address and prayer, this age is assumed by many, without question, to be the kingdom of Christ; though no Scripture is found to warrant that conclusion.*[8]

A LIGHT TO THE WORLD

After pleading with his Jewish brother to come to Jesus so that he may bring the kingdom (Acts 3:17–21), Peter referenced the Torah in Acts 3:22–23:

> Moses said, 'The Lord God will raise up for you a prophet like me from your brothers. You shall listen to him in whatever he tells you. And it shall be that every soul who does not listen to that prophet shall be destroyed from the people.'

Moses prophesied that a prophet would arise that was like him (Deut 18:15–19), likely meaning that he would be a deliverer, lawgiver, and head

---

8. Chafer, *Satan*, 29.

of the nation. The prophecy was well known by Jews at the time, for they were looking for this prophet to arrive (John 1:21, 25; 7:40). Peter's sermon confirmed that this prophet is Jesus. This means that from the time of Moses until Jesus, the kingdom in Israel could not have reached its sublime state. Israel failed as a kingdom of priests because she could not obey on her own. She did and still does need the Messiah to do the job.

The Millennium is, then, a necessary period in the saga of the kingdom. It is the prophetic climax of God's overarching redemptive agenda. His completed promises to Israel, found in the unconditional covenants, will be on full display before a world of believers and unbelievers alike. A holy Israel will shine in the midst of a world needing to know God. This is a purpose that could never be achieved in the Eternal State because all the inhabitants will already know their Creator. Once Israel is empowered to obey God through an intimate relationship with Jesus, his desired role for the nation will be realized. She will be set high above all the nations of the earth (Deut 28:1; cf. Isa 2:2–4; Mic 4:1–3), as the head and not the tail (Deut 28:13). Had God simply raised up Israel to her ideal state immediately, the Jewish people would not have as much reason to worship him. Only after thousands of years of Israel trying and failing to be a light to the world will she be able to truly appreciate the Messiah's redemptive work. When Israel does become a light to the world, it will not be as the source, but as a reflection of the LORD's glory. The glory of Jesus will shine before the world as nations will be drawn to his light and kings to his brightness (Isa 60:1–3; cf. 49:6; Zech 8:22–23).

This chapter was only a survey and a brief history of the kingdom. Alva McClain's, *The Greatness of the Kingdom: An Inductive Study of the Kingdom of God*, is highly recommended for further study.

4

The Road to Eden

THERE ARE TWO KEY points regarding the nature of the Millennium that Revelation 20:1–7 teaches us. First, Jesus will be reigning with his saints (vv. 4, 6). Second, Satan will be bound (vv. 2–3; 7). The binding of Satan is not to be understood as merely a limitation on his power. Satan will no longer be able to deceive the nations because he and the other rebel angels will have been thrown into the abyss (v. 3; Isa 24:21–22; cf. Luke 8:31). There will, however, still be sinners and death in the Millennium (Isa 65:20; Zech 14:17). This suggests that the Millennium is a transitional period transpiring before the perfection to be found in the Eternal State. With Jesus reigning on the earth and Satan being bound, it is easy to understand why this will be an age of wonders. The artistry of the Millennium is not limited to the spiritual. Geography, ecology, and healthcare are all radically changed on the road to Eden.

GEOGRAPHY

At the Second Coming of the Messiah, the first place his feet will touch the earth will be atop the Mount of Olives (Zech 14:4; Acts 1:11–12). This will result in the Mount of Olives being split in two. One half of the mountain will move northward and the other southward. This will provide a large valley through which surviving Jews from the final battle of Armageddon may flee (Zech 14:4–5). This earthquake is connected to the one brought about as a result of God coming against Gog and to the seventh bowl judgment. Every man and animal on the earth will feel the earth shake as islands are drowned and mountains are reduced to rubble (Ezek 38:18–20; Rev 16:18–20). The seventh bowl judgment occurs shortly before the inauguration of the Millennium. Therefore, at least some of the topographical changes that exist in the Millennium are the result of God's judgments at the end of the current age.

The Millennial River

The valley formed by the splitting of the Mount of Olives will make a path for an amazing river that will flow during the Millennium. The river's fountainhead will be in the house of the LORD (Joel 3:18). Specifically, it will stream from below the temple's threshold facing the east (Ezek 47:1). The river begins as only a trickle of water on the south side (Ezek 47:2). As it moves eastward the river will become progressively deeper. The river's depth builds from ankle deep to knee deep to waist deep until it finally becomes so wide and deep that a man could swim in it but be unable to ford. These four deviations are measured in sets of 1,750 feet (Ezek 47:2–5). In total, they represent the distance from Jerusalem to the eastern slope of the Mount of Olives.

The river flows in two directions, to the eastern sea (the Dead Sea) and to the western sea (the Mediterranean) (Zech 14:8). The result is a sort of double river. Wherever the waters flow there will be life as a result (Ezek 47:9). A more literal translation of Ezekiel 47:9 reads, *And wherever the two rivers go . . .* While most of the biblical narrative covers the eastern side of the river, the characteristics of the western side can be inferred.

Several species of fruit trees will grow alongside the banks of the millennial river. These trees will never fail to produce vibrant fruit. A different species will grow every month. In addition, the leaves of the trees will never wither and will be used for medicine (Ezek 47:7, 12). The abilities of these trees mark them as unlike anything that has grown since the fall of man. They are the direct result of the river that flows from the sanctuary (Ezek 47:12).

The river will hold such an inherent healing effect that that Dead Sea will require a name change. Ezekiel 47:8–11:

> *And he said to me, "This water flows toward the eastern region and goes down into the Arabah, and enters the sea; when the water flows into the sea, the water will become fresh. And wherever the river goes, every living creature that swarms will live, and there will be*

very many fish. For this water goes there, that the waters of the sea may become fresh; so everything will live where the river goes. Fisherman will stand beside the sea. From Engedi to Eneglaim it will be a place for the spreading of nets. Its fish will be of very many kinds, like fish of the Great Sea. But its swamps and marshes will not become fresh.

The river will pour into the Arabah[1] and will make fresh what was once among the saltiest bodies of water on the earth (v. 8). At present the Dead Sea is so inhospitable that only a few forms of microorganisms can survive in it. The Hebrew *Yam haMavet* could even be translated as *killer sea*. The sea means death to any fish unfortunate enough find his way into the water. When the healing powers of the millennial river cascade into the Arabah the status quo is bound to change. Wherever the river goes there will be life and an abundance of fish (v. 9), including what will then become the living sea. It is of no great mystery as to why the psalmist says that this river will make the city of God glad (Ps 46:4). The river will pass through Engedi and Eneglaim,[2] for men will spread their nets to catch fish from these locations (v. 10). There will be so many fish caught, representing so many species, that for the purposes of fishing the Dead Sea will become like the Mediterranean (v. 10).

In contrast to these changes, there will be left some swamps and marshes that will not become fresh (v. 11). The remaining salted areas are emblematic of the transitional nature of the Millennium. The saltiness of the Dead Sea can rightly be understood to symbolize death. Even with Jesus reigning from David's throne there will still be death, though it be diminished (cf. Isa 65:20). Great improvements will have been made, but perfection is yet to be found after the Millennium, in the Eternal State.

Indeed, the millennial river itself serves as a fine example of something that is in a transitional stage. The river continues to flow in the Eternal State but is improved beyond its already impressive character. In the New Jerusalem there will be a river, clear as crystal, flowing from the Lamb's throne (Rev 22:1). This is the perfected version of the water coming from under the threshold of the temple (Ezek 47:1, Joel 3:18). In the New Jerusalem there is no temple, for the Lord God and the Lamb are the archetype of the

1. The Arabah is the hollow depression that extends from the Sea of Galilee to the Gulf of Aqabah.

2. The location of Eneglaim is unknown, though it likely rests somewhere near Qumran on the northwestern shore of the Dead Sea.

various temples (John 2:21; Rev 21:22). The Lamb's river flows down the middle of the street and on each side there are trees of life, bearing twelve kinds of fruit every month. Just like the millennial river, the Lamb's river will also produce trees that grow leaves for healing. But the trees growing along the Lamb's river are each referred to as the tree of life (Rev 22:2). This is no minor distinction as to eat from such a tree results in eternal life (Gen 3:22). It is possible that the trees on the banks of the millennial river are also trees of life, though the text is not so specific. Regardless, the millennial river will be upgraded or replaced by one that is far superior.

The Jerusalem Mountain

During the Millennium, the land surrounding Jerusalem will have been transformed into a plain. It will run from Geba in the north to Rimmon in the South (Zech 14:10).[3] The plain will contrast with the then highly lifted Jerusalem and King Jesus who will be ruling from the summit (Zech 14:9–10). Jerusalem's mountain will be established as the highest of the mountains and shall be raised higher than the hills. The mountain's great height emphasizes Jerusalem as the center of world authority, for all of the nations will flow to it (Isa 2:2; Mic 4:1). The temple sitting on the top will be a house or prayer for all nations (Isa 56:7). Because the mountain serves to lift up a city, the temple, and the surrounding land, the summit is a plateau almost fifty miles in length (Ezek 40:5; 45:1; 48:8).[4]

Because the mountains of the earth will have been made low, we do not know how high Jerusalem's mountain will rise. If it does reach the current height of Everest, or that of a number of other shorter but still towering mountains, then one would assume the conditions near the summit would be rather harsh. However, not only is there land there set aside for farming (Ezek 48:18–19), but the prophet also spoke of a majestic tree in Ezekiel 17:22–24:

> Thus says the Lord GOD: "I myself will take a sprig from the lofty top of the cedar and will set it out. I will break off from the topmost of its young twigs a tender one, and I myself will plant it on a high and lofty mountain. On the mountain height of Israel will I plant it, that it may bear branches and produce fruit and become a noble

3. Geba is located approximately six miles NE of Jerusalem, while Rimmon is thirty-five miles SW.

4. 25,000 reeds is the equivalent of 49.8 miles.

cedar. And under it will dwell every kind of bird; in the shade of its branches birds of every sort will nest. And all the trees of the field shall know that I am the LORD; I bring low the high tree, and make high the low tree, dry up the green tree, and make the dry tree flourish. I am the LORD; I have spoken, and I will do it.[5]

No trees, including the cedar, grow atop the highest mountains on the earth. This will change when God transplants a piece of a cedar from its mother tree and places it on the height of Jerusalem's millennial mountain (vv. 22–23). The Hebrew for cedar here is *'erez*. It describes any kind of coniferous or pine tree. Cedars are not known for their ability to produce fruit. This will change in the Millennium as at least one conifer will yield such produce. This is just one of the reasons that the cedar atop Jerusalem's mountain will be referred to as noble. Further nobility comes from its significance in height and canopy. Both will provide enough room and shade to house every kind of bird (v.23).

The final verse reveals God's purpose behind the tree: to provide a stark contrast with the other trees of the fields. The transplant also exemplifies the ability of God to modify the forestry of the earth. All of the trees are subject to God's will. The highest of trees can be brought low, while the lowest may be raised high. God can wither the lush and revive the desiccated (cf. Matt 21:18–19). The highest mountain on earth will not be covered with snow. Rather, it will be a place where the most opulent of plant life will flourish. The LORD has spoken, and he will bring about all of these marvels (v. 24). The cedar may be a millennial version of the Tree of Life. The fruit producing evergreen may also be a physical representation of the LORD himself (cf. Hos 14:8). He will be a perennial presence among his people and the sole source of their blessings.

ECOLOGY

Animals and Man in Harmony

Much of the Millennium's ecology can be understood from even a cursory reading of Isaiah 11:6–9:

---

5. Ezekiel described the greatness of Assyria's former state by comparing it to a similar cedar of great height and breadth (Ezek 31:3–9). The prophet used metaphor in picturing Assyria with the future glory of Jerusalem likely in mind.

The wolf shall dwell with the lamb, and the leopard shall lie down with the young goat, and the calf and the lion and the fattened calf together; and a little child shall lead them. The cow and the bear shall graze; their young shall lie down together; and the lion shall eat straw like the ox. The nursing child shall play over the hole of the cobra, and the weaned child shall put his hand on the adder's den. They shall not hurt or destroy in all my holy mountain; for the earth shall be full of the knowledge of the LORD as the waters cover the sea.

Several pairings are described as being in a state of peace with one another. The seeming repetition of this principle is not only for emphasis. There are a few things that can be asserted regarding the overall nature of the Millennium. There will no longer be predators in the animal kingdom. The former hunter and hunted will live and sleep among each other (v. 6). People will be able to live securely in the wilderness and sleep in the woods (Ezek 34:25). A little boy being able to lead animals and animals being prevented from harming children, indicates that humanity will regain its complete dominion over all the earth (vv. 6; 8; cf. Gen 1:26). Humanity lost some of its control to Satan when Adam sinned (Gen 3:17–19; cf. 2 Cor 4:4; Eph 2:2). During the Millennium, Satan will be bound, no longer having any influence.

Carnivores will be made into herbivores (v. 7). This newfound vegetarianism is the reason for animals no longer preying on one another (v. 9), for the plowman will overtake the reaper (Amos 9:13). This is an Edenic principle generally being put into effect in that men and animals were originally given only plants to eat (Gen 1:29–30). Animal flesh will still be consumed by some people, notably as part of temple worship (Ezek 44–46). People will also eat fish (Ezek 47:10), which is a different kind of flesh (1 Cor 15:39). The resurrected Jesus still ate fish (Luke 24:42–43). The change in ecology is attributed to the earth being filled with the knowledge of the LORD. The filling will be so comprehensive that it is compared to the level by which the waters cover the sea (v. 9; Hab 2:14). Knowledge does not typically influence those things that lack a mind so directly. God's overwhelming knowledge will do so in the Millennium, modifying creation into a harmonious state (cf. Rom 8:18–22).

Increased Blessings from the Land

Astonishingly, this level of harmony is to such a degree that mountains will break into shouts of joy, blooming deserts will sing, and the trees and rivers will clap their hands (Ps 98:8; Isa 35:1–2; 55:12). Even some premillennialists believe that this type of prophecy is only a general description of millennial blessings. However, there is no reason to doubt that this prophecy is essentially literal, whereas there is good reason to affirm it. The trees may not exactly be banging their branches together, but nature producing songs of joy in some sense is to be expected. Creation finally being freed from her subjection to futility (Rom 8:20) would surely be an occasion to sing. Through the power of God even stones may cry out (Luke 19:40). Jesus caused a fig tree to wither because it would not produce fruit (Matt 21:19). He will replace the thorns with the cypress and the myrtle (Isa 55:13). Created things either serve God or die. Nature will not only serve the Messiah, but do so unlike any time since before the fall. It is safe to assume that all theologians to one extent or another are underestimating the wonders to be found in the Millennial Kingdom.

Isaiah 35 is entirely devoted to the Millennium, with much of the narrative on a rejuvenated wilderness. Here we find that the desert will be glad and the Arabah will rejoice and blossom abundantly like the crocus (vv. 1–2). The crocus is among the first types of flowers to bloom in the spring, at times even arising out of the snow. Isaiah described a period where previously desolate land now not only produces, but does so early in the year. Even the deserts will be able to support an abundance of life as they will become springs of water (v. 7).

In general, the land across the planet will produce food in a way that that none on earth have experienced since Adam and Eve's exit from paradise. Naturally, Israel will enjoy the greatest level of production. Those who pass by Israel will be so impressed by the change in ecology that they will compare her to the Garden of Eden (Ezek 36:34–35). Israel is to become such a renowned place for planting crops that there will be no famine in the land (Ezek 34:29). The land even benefits from rain falling at determined times instead of the randomness that leads to floods and drought (Ezek 34:26). The Israelites shall plant vineyards and gardens and enjoy their wine and fruit (Jer 31:5; Amos 9:14). Israel will produce such a surplus that she will fill the whole world with her fruit (Isa 27:6).

The production and quality of grapes reaching astonishing levels is a specific example. When Moses sent spies to investigate Canaan they came to the Wadi of Eshcol.[6] It was there that the spies retrieved a single cluster of grapes so large that it had to be carried on a pole by two men (Num 13:23). This was a free sample of what the Hebrews can expect from the Holy Land once they dwell there in obedience (Ezek 34:27). This famous cluster of grapes is going to seem tiny compared to those harvested in the Millennium. Wine will become so plentiful that it is described as dripping from the mountains and flowing from the hills (Joel 3:18, Amos 9:13). An abundance of wine in the Millennium is to be expected, for Jesus told his disciples that he would drink from the fruit of the vine with them in the coming kingdom (Matt 26:29).

WASTELANDS

Babylon

Not every place on earth is going to become more like Eden. In addition to the marshes of the Dead Sea remaining salty and lifeless (Ezek 47:11), some areas of the earth will become nothing but desolate wastelands. One such wasteland is Babylon in modern-day Iraq. Isaiah 13:19–22:

> And Babylon, the glory of kingdoms, the splendor and pomp of the Chaldeans, will be like Sodom and Gomorrah when God overthrew them. It will never be inhabited or lived in for all generations; no Arab will pitch his tent there; no shepherds will make their flocks lie down there. But wild animals will lie down there, and their houses will be full of howling creatures; there ostriches will dwell, and there wild goats will dance. Hyenas will cry in its towers, and jackals in the pleasant palaces; its time is close at hand and its days will not be prolonged.

Jeremiah confirmed that Babylon will suffer the same fate as Sodom and Gomorrah and will only be inhabited by wild beasts (Jer 50:39–40). These beasts are actually demons with animal characteristics (Rev 18:2). Babylon, once the praise of the whole earth, will become a horror among the nations.

---

6. A wadi is a dried river bed. Eschol means *cluster*. To this day the Wadi of Eshcol is renowned for its grapes.

Her land will become so parched that men will not even pass through, let alone live there (Jer 51:41–43). Throughout the Millennium, smoke will perpetually rise from the ruined city (Rev 19:3). Once home to one of the Seven Wonders of the Ancient World, Babylon will never see her hanging gardens again.

Edom

Another significant wasteland is Edom in southern Jordan. The most comprehensive description of the city's future condition is found in Isaiah 34:8–15:

> For the LORD has a day of vengeance, a year of recompense for the cause of Zion. And the streams of Edom shall be turned into pitch, and her soil into sulfur; her land shall become burning pitch. Night and day it shall not be quenched; its smoke shall go up forever. From generation to generation it shall lie waste; none shall pass through it forever and ever. But the hawk and the porcupine shall possess it, the owl and the raven shall dwell in it. He shall stretch the line of confusion over it, and the plumb line of emptiness. Its nobles—there is no one there to call it a kingdom, and all its princes shall be nothing. Thorns shall grow over its strongholds, nettles and thistles in its fortresses. It shall be the haunt of jackals, an abode for ostriches. And wild animals shall meet with hyenas; the wild goat shall cry to his fellow; indeed, there the night bird settles and finds for herself a resting place. There the owl nests and lays and hatches and gathers her young in her shadow; indeed, there the hawks are gathered, each one with her mate.

As expected, Edom's condition will match that of Babylon's. She too will be compared to Sodom and Gomorrah (Jer 49:18). Her devastation is the result of God avenging Israel (v. 8; cf. Obad 1:10). The land, streams, and air will become so poisoned that men will be unable to pass through. Smoke will continue to rise from Edom until the end of this world (vv. 9–10). Just as in Babylon, many animals representing various kinds of demons[7] will inhabit the sulfuric Edom (vv. 11; 14–15). Thorns and thistles growing over Edom's strongholds (v. 14) signal that this area will be under the control of

---

7. The Hebrew *Lilith*, translated as *night bird* in Isaiah 34:14, is more literally translated as *night monster*. Likewise, the Hebrew *Sa`iyr*, translated as *wild goat*, more specifically identifies a goat-like demon.

sin (Gen 3:17–18). This is in contrast to the majority of the earth being free from such growth (Isa 55:13).

The prophet gave us more details on why Edom is to be devastated and poisoned in Ezekiel 35:9–15. Her people conspired to take the land of Israel and Judah after their desolation (v. 10). Edom disparaged Israel, rejoiced over the fall of Judah, and spoke arrogantly against the LORD (vv. 12–13). As a result, he kept his promise to Abram and cursed those who cursed Israel (Gen 12:3). Just as Edom spoke against the mountains of Israel and celebrated the desolation of Judah (v. 12), the world will celebrate the desolation of Mount Seir and all of Edom (vv. 14–15).

The permanence of Edom's desolation is important to note. Joel 3:19:

> "Egypt shall become a desolation and Edom a desolate wilderness,
> for the violence done to the people of Judah, because they have shed
> innocent blood in their land.

We know that Egypt's desolation will only last forty years (Ezek 29:12). At some point in the Millennium, God will even consider Egypt to be his people (Isa 19:25). In contrast, Edom will remain a place of perpetual desolation for shedding the blood of the Jews in their own land.

The subjugation of the Edomites by the Babylonians, the Medo-Persians, and John Hyrcanus the Hasmonean in 126 BC, has led to their end as a distinct people. Their cities have become nothing more than ruins, just as prophesied (Jer 49:13). These facts would seem to suggest the fulfillment of Edom's desolation. However, the level of destruction and the presence of demons, as recorded in Isaiah, has not yet been reached. A future execution of judgment in the region is to be expected. When he returns, the Messiah will pour out his wrath upon those gathered against him in Bozrah, the capital of Edom (Isa 63:1–6; cf. Rev 19:13–15).

Hells on Earth

The descriptions of Babylon and Edom as being filled with smoke, sulfur, pitch, and demons make them little hells on earth. They offer a stark contrast to an otherwise beautified world. The prophets made it a point to stress this contrast. The Messianic Kingdom will be filled with princes while Edom will have no kingdom and no princes (Isa 34:12). While the entire earth rejoices, Edom will be made into a wasteland (Ezek 35:14). Those passing by Israel will compare her to the Garden of Eden (Ezek 36:34–35), while those passing by Edom and Babylon will be horrified and hiss (Jer 49:17; 51:41–43). These are instructive juxtapositions that speak to the very essence of the Millennium. It is to be a golden age that is in many ways Edenic. However, only in the Eternal State will everything be made perfect.

HEALTHCARE

Increased blessings from the land alone would be enough to postulate that the health of humanity will be improved. But the root cause should always be in the forefront of the reader's mind. In the Millennium there is a momentous force that will radically augment the vigor of mankind: Jesus Christ. The physical presence of the Messiah will promote miraculous health. During the first advent, many people came to hear Jesus and be healed of their infirmities and demonic influences. These individuals were trying to make physical contact with Jesus because healing power was pouring from him (e.g., Luke 6:19). Jesus was such a well of healing that he did not even have to seek to restore a person. There was a woman who was healed of a hemorrhage because she merely touched the fringe of Jesus' cloak. Jesus perceived that he had been touched because power came out of him (Luke 8:43–46). It is critical to understand that power only came out of Jesus because the woman had faith (Luke 8:48). This will change to a degree in the Millennium, as even those who do not trust in Jesus as Lord and Savior will nevertheless reap health benefits from his presence.

Isaiah 65:17–25 is a beautiful summary of the characteristics of the kingdom, including the Eternal State but with a focus on the Messianic Age. God promised that he will create new heavens and a new earth (v. 17). Before this can come to pass, there must first be a transition. Just as Pentecost ushered in the age between the First and Second Coming (Acts 2:17), the Millennium will usher in the Eternal State. Verses 20–23:

> *No more shall there be in it an infant who lives but a few days, or an old man who does not fill out his days, for the young man shall die a hundred years old, and the sinner a hundred years old shall be accursed. They shall build houses and inhabit them; they shall plant vineyards and eat their fruit. They shall not build and another inhabit; they shall not plant and another eat; for like the days of a tree shall the days of my people be, and my chosen shall long enjoy the work of their hands. They shall not labor in vain or bear children for calamity, for they shall be the offspring of the blessed of the LORD, and their descendants with them.*

The remarkable lifespans enjoyed during the antediluvian period will return (cf. Gen 5). Babies will no longer be born only to soon after perish, nor will any mother face the grief of bearing a stillborn child. If a man builds a home then he will get to inhabit it for as long as it stands. If he plants a vineyard or a tree then he will get to eat from them for as long as they grow. Even sinners can expect to possess what would currently be considered a full life, consisting of at least one hundred years. But in the Millennium, those who were only able to become mere centenarians will have died at such a young age that they will be regarded as accursed. The wages of sin will always be death (Rom 6:23).

Adam Died in that Millennium

God told Adam that in the day that he ate of the tree of knowledge of good and evil, he would surely die (Gen 2:17). Adam did eat of the tree (Gen 3:6), and nevertheless went on to live to the ripe old age of 930 years (Gen 5:5). The most common modern explanation for this is that God meant that Adam would die a spiritual death in that day. No doubt that Adam's sin resulted in a spiritual death (cf. Ezek 18:20; Rom 5:12; Eph 2:1). The problem with limiting this death to the spirit is that God told Adam that because he had eaten of the tree that his body would return to dust (Gen 3:17–19), signifying a physical death. There is another possibility as to why Adam lived for many days after eating of the forbidden fruit. Perhaps Adam died not in that *day*, indicating a twenty-four hour period,[8] but in that *day*, indicating an epoch, or more specifically, a millennium. The latter option is the older of interpretations.

The Book of Jubilees is an ancient Hebrew work that is also known as *Lesser Genesis*, due to its extensive commentary on Genesis. Jubilees is included in the Dead Sea Scrolls and dates to at least 200 BC.[9] Jubilees was not included in the canon and is therefore not authoritative. It was, however, well known among the early Christians and is mentioned by name or alluded to in many of their writings. The treatise is a reliable historic source

8. The use of *day* in Genesis 2:17 is not bookended by references to evening and morning that clarify the meaning of *day* that is found several times in the six days of creation (Gen 1).

9. The Book of Jubilees alludes to 1 Enoch's *Book of Dreams*; of which a Dead Sea Scroll copy has been carbon dated to ca. 200 BC.

for the purpose of investigating how both ancient Hebrews and Christians understood Genesis 2:17.

Consider Jubilees 4:29–30:

> ... he was the first to be buried in the ground. He lacked seventy years of one thousand years, for a thousand years are one day in the testimony of heaven. Therefore it is written about the tree of knowledge: "For on the day you eat from it, you shall die." Therefore he did not complete the years of this day because he died during it.[10]

Explained here is that a thousand years are as one day in the testimony of heaven, i.e., God's perspective. Moses, the author of Genesis, corroborated this line of thinking by connecting man returning to dust with the revelation that a thousand years in God's sight are as yesterday when it is past (Ps 90:3–4). The apostle Peter also taught that with the Lord one day is as a thousand years, and a thousand years are as one day (2 Pet 3:8). Adam died seventy years short of a full thousand. The author of Jubilees deduced that because Adam ate of the Tree of Knowledge, he died in that millennial day.

This interpretation of the meaning of *day* in Genesis 2:17 was not limited to the ancient Hebrews. The very same conclusion regarding just when Adam died from eating the fruit was present in the early church. Prominent ante-Nicene church-father Justin Martyr confessed:

> Now we have understood that the expression used among these words, 'According to the days of the tree [of life] shall be the days of my people; the works of their toil shall abound' obscurely predicts a thousand years. For as Adam was told that in the day he ate of the tree he would die, we know that he did not complete a thousand years. We have perceived, moreover, that the expression, 'The day of the Lord is as a thousand years,' is connected with this subject.[11]

The chapter that this quote is taken from is entirely devoted to how the Millennial Kingdom relates to Genesis 2:17; 3, and Isaiah 65:17–25. Justin understood that the latter passage was concerned with fixing the damage that was inflicted in the former two. The father connected the narratives to such a degree that he even identified the tree mentioned in Isaiah 65:22 as the Tree of Life.[12] An astute observation as the verse also suggests that

10. Wise et al., *Dead Sea Scrolls*, 322–323.

11. Roberts et al., *Ante-Nicene Fathers Volume I*, 239. Justin Martyr, *Dialogue with Trypho*, Chapter LXXXI.

12. The Targumim, Septuagint, and Arabic translations render the reference to a tree in Isaiah 65:22, *as the days of the tree of life*.

the inefficient working of the soil will come to an end. This is the reversal of Adam being forced out of the Garden to work the soil so that he would no longer have access to the Tree of Life (Gen 3:22–23). Justin explained that Isaiah 65:22 predicts the Millennium by linking the verse to Adam's inability to live a full thousand years. If Adam had not been exiled from the Garden then he would have possessed the lifetime found in the Tree, lasting an infinite amount of days in any respect. Among others, Justin understood that this was connected to the expression that the day of the Lord is as a thousand years (2 Pet 3:8–10).

Even if the *day* in Genesis 2:17 was a literal twenty-four hour period and the death was a spiritual one only, Adam dying in the first millennium still has great significance. Adam was created as an immortal. And yet, because Adam sinned his body was consigned to the earth before even a mere thousand years were completed. All of humanity inherited Adam's sin (Rom 5:12), likewise reaping both spiritual and physical death. Not even Methuselah lived a full millennium (Gen 5:27). The long lifespans in the period between the fall and the flood reveal a transition away from Eden. The long lifespans between the return of Jesus and the Eternal State reveal a transition back to Eden. Man living throughout the entire millennial reign of Jesus will testify that the fall of Adam has been overcome. The first millennium was marked by death while the last will be marked by life.

ISRAEL IS EDEN

There is a simple reason why much of the narrative concerning restoration in the Millennium alludes to both the land of Israel and Eden: the land of Israel is Eden. Specifically, Israel is likely located where Eden once was. Likewise, Jerusalem is likely located in the center of where the Garden of Eden once was.

Many traditionally think of the Garden of Eden as having been located in Mesopotamia because the Tigris and Euphrates rivers are mentioned (Gen 2:14). However, these rivers are only ever said to be flowing out of the greater territory of Eden and not necessarily in the Garden. The rivers were just two of four that all branched off from one (Gen 2:10–14).[13] The Pishon and Gihon rivers apparently no longer exist. It could be that the two sides of the millennial river represent the return of these missing rivers

13. The grammar of Genesis 2:10 makes it unclear as to whether the rivers diverged at the Garden or elsewhere in Eden.

in Eden. In any case, no topography in Mesopotamia or Israel currently matches the biblical description. Over thousands of years there have been geographical changes to the Fertile Crescent that render Moses' identification of the Garden's location problematic. The issue has to be considered through other avenues.

Navel of the World

Jerusalem is referred to as the *navel* of the world in the Septuagint translation of Judges 9:37 and in the literal translation of Ezekiel 38:12. A navel indicates a center or middle, and that is how most modern translations render the verses. Primarily, the navel is the point at which the umbilical cord is or was attached to an organism. As the navel of the world, Jerusalem is both at the center of the nations and where God first provided nourishment and life. With this in mind, it makes all the more sense that Israel is a channel through which blessing comes to the rest of the world (e.g., Gen 12:3; Isa 19:24; Zech 8:13). Jerusalem is also referred to as the *apple of his eye*, meaning that she is cherished by God above all other cities and nations (Zech 2:8). The logic behind the terms *navel of the world* and *apple of his eye* could also be applied to the Garden of Eden.

In the Beginning was the Word in Eden

That the Son of God walked in Eden is based on Genesis 3:8:

> And they heard the sound of the LORD God walking in the garden in the cool of the day, and the man and his wife hid themselves from the presence of the LORD God among the trees of the garden.

When reading this verse in English it seems only natural to conclude that Adam and Eve heard the sound created by the LORD walking in the garden. The Hebrew allows for a far more profound possibility. This is that Adam and Eve heard the sound itself walking in the garden. The English above allows for this understanding as well if the verse is read carefully and if conclusions, albeit understandable ones, are not jumped to. Some translations, such as the Authorized King James, render the Hebrew *qowl* as *voice* instead of *sound*, providing some helpful nuance. The interpretation of the walking sound, voice, or word is so old that it is likely to be the original.

The Targum Onkelos version of Genesis 3:8:

*And they heard the voice of the Word of the Lord God walking in
the garden in the evening of the day; and Adam and his wife hid
themselves from before the Lord God among the trees of the garden.*

Targumim (singular: *Targum*) are Aramaic renderings of Hebrew Scripture, some dating from at least the time of Ezra (ca. 458 BC). The Targumim are often not so much word-for-word translations, but are expository
paraphrases that were intended to teach the audience truths or nuances
that would be otherwise missed by the layman. In the case of Genesis 3:8,
the word *Word* was added. This was done to make it clear that it was the
Word of the LORD that was heard walking and not the sound made by
the LORD walking. The Aramaic for *word* in this verse is *memra*; it is the
equivalent of *logos* in the Greek.

The apostle John famously identified the *Logos* as Jesus in John 1:1
and 1:14:

*In the beginning was the Word, and the Word was with God, and
the Word was God.*

*And the Word became flesh and dwelt among us, and we have seen
his glory, glory as of the only Son from the Father, full of grace and
truth.*

Surely the Word of the LORD God *in* Genesis 3:8 is the same as the Word
that was with God and was God. It is, after all, the role of the Son to reveal God before man (John 1:18). Therefore, it was the pre-incarnate Jesus
that Adam and Eve heard walking in Eden. Jesus called to man, and in response Adam and Eve hid themselves from his presence because they were
ashamed of their now realized nudity (Gen 3:8–10). It is unlikely that the
LORD would only chose to fellowship with Adam and Eve after they had
sinned. The implication is that he regularly strolled through the Garden,
perhaps customarily in the evening.

Before the fall, the LORD apparently made the Garden of Eden his
regular place of terrestrial habitation. After the fall, the LORD made it clear
that he desires to dwell in Jerusalem and will do so forever (Ps 132:13–14).
This continues in the Millennium and forever afterward, at which time
King Jesus will be ruling from Jerusalem (e.g., Isa 24:23). If Jerusalem is not
located where the Garden of Eden once was, then God has changed where
he makes his home on earth. If Jerusalem is located where the Garden once
was, then God has not changed his residence. The second possibility is

more in keeping with God's immutable nature (e.g., 1 Sam 15:29; Heb 13:8; Jas 1:17).

The Garden of Eden was a Copy

The holy buildings and items made by the hands of men were copies of the true things found in Heaven (Heb 9:23–24). God instructed Moses to have the Tabernacle and all of its furniture constructed based on the pattern he was shown on the mountain (Exod 25:8–9; 26:30). Highly specific instructions were given because God needed a dwelling place among men. Presumably, God wanted a home on earth that was reminiscent of his home in Heaven. The true tabernacle was raised by the Lord in Heaven (Heb 8:1–2; Rev 15:5). There is also an original temple in Heaven and within it is the original Ark of the Covenant (Rev 11:19).

This same relationship applies to the Garden of Eden. The most notable object within the Garden of Eden was the Tree of Life (Gen 2:9). The New Jerusalem is currently located in Heaven (Gal 4:26; Rev 21:2) and is home to the Tree of Life (Rev 22:2). The faithful are promised that they shall eat of the Tree of Life located in this true garden of God (Rev 2:7). Man was cast from the Garden and blocked from access to the Tree of Life by cherubim and a flaming sword (Gen 3:24). The saints are to be blessed by entering through the gates of the New Jerusalem, having a right to the Tree of Life (Rev 22:14). The Garden of Eden was, then, patterned after the Jerusalem in Heaven. It would seem that the earthly Jerusalem is located where the Garden of Eden once was.

Two Options

In addition to the aforementioned comparison of Israel to the Garden of Eden in Ezekiel 36:34–35, we have Isaiah 51:3:

> For the LORD comforts Zion; he comforts all her waste places and makes her wilderness like Eden, her desert like the garden of the LORD; joy and gladness will be found in her, thanksgiving and the voice of song.

During the Millennium, the Promised Land will be nearly restored. At that time, her wilderness will be like Eden and her desert like the Garden. This provides us with two options. Either the LORD is going to restructure the land of Israel to become like Eden once was, or the LORD is going to re-store the land of Israel back to its original state of actually being Eden. If the second option is not the case then there will effectively be two Edens on earth. For a restoration of creation would include something as significant as Eden. In utilizing Occam's razor we can reasonably assume that Eden and Israel share the same site. Whether you believe Israel was the actual location of Eden or not, it is clear that the promised future restoration of Israel bears the earmarks of a paradise restored, of a new Eden.

THE TRIUMPH OF THE LAST ADAM

The fall initiated by Adam was so severe that it harmed not just mankind but all of creation (Gen 3:17–19; Rom 8:19–20). Adam's disobedience brought sin to the world, whereas Jesus' obedience brought righteousness (Rom 5:19). The juxtaposition between the destroyer and the Restorer pro-vides a contrast like no other. Jesus could not truly be the last Adam (1 Cor 15:45) if he did not fully repair both the spiritual and the physical damage wrought by the first Adam. Jesus absolutely repaired the spiritual damage with his death on the cross (John 19:30). The same line of thinking should lead the saint to conclude that Jesus will also repair the physical damage inflicted on mankind and creation.

The language of the fall was alluded to in several passages on the resto-ration. For example, compare Genesis 3:17–18 with Isaiah 55:13:

> And to Adam he said, "Because you have listened to the voice of your wife and have eaten of the tree of which I commanded you, 'You shall not eat of it,' cursed is the ground because of you; in pain you shall eat of it all the days of your life; thorns and thistles it shall bring forth for you; and you shall eat the plants of the field.

> Instead of the thorn shall come up the cypress; instead of the brier shall come up the myrtle; and it shall make a name for the LORD, an everlasting sign that shall not be cut off."

Even the ground became cursed as a result of Adam's sin. Though this re-sulted in all plant life becoming likewise impaired, the sign of the curse was that now thorns and thistles grew. This sign of sin appears several times in Scripture, most notably on the head of Jesus during his passion (e.g., John 19:5). In Isaiah we see that the thorn producing plants will be replaced with the myrtle and the cypress. There were no thorns growing before the fall, nor will they be permitted in most areas in the Millennium. This will make a name for the LORD and be an everlasting sign that sin has been defeated.

Refreshing and Restoration

Soon after the birth of the Body of Christ at Pentecost (Acts 2), Peter addressed his fellow Jews from Solomon's Portico in Acts 3:19–21:

> Repent therefore, and turn back, that your sins may be blotted out, that times of refreshing may come from the presence of the Lord, and that he may send the Christ appointed for you, Jesus, whom heaven must receive until the time for restoring all the things about which God spoke by the mouth of his holy prophets long ago.

When the Jews turn from their sin of rejecting Jesus as Messiah they will experience times of refreshing (v. 20) and restoration (v. 21). All of the covenants, promises, and prophecies yet to be fulfilled will finally become so after Jesus returns from Heaven (v.21). The Greek word behind *restoring* here is *apokatastasis*. It is only used once in the New Testament, and is deep in its meaning. The *apokatastasis* goes beyond indicating a general restitution, but specifically includes the return of the kingdom to Israel (Acts 1:6–7) and a return to Eden. The restoration of the kingdom works in concert with the restoration of creation. God spoke of this moment by the mouth of his holy prophets from ancient times (v. 21).

Because a transitional period toward the restoration of Eden is fundamental to the Millennium's nature, it is only fitting that Satan will be bound for the duration (Rev 20:2–3). This time there will be no serpent to tempt man out of Eden. Satan may have defeated the first Adam but certainly not the last.

5

Millennial Government

WORSHIP AND GOVERNMENT ARE so intrinsically connected during the Millennium that it is difficult to consider one without looking to the other. At times the overlap is to such a degree that worship is indistinguishable from government. This is a concept divorced from many modern societies, though it was not always. With God in the person of Jesus reigning over the entire planet, both spiritually and physically, it only follows that his government would serve to bring him honor and praise.

THE POPULATION

Necessary to understanding why the government and system of worship operate as they do, is the identification of the two classes of people who will populate the Millennium. The first class is comprised of those with glorified bodies. Upon death, the believer is taken to paradise (Luke 23:43); to be away from the body is to be with the Lord (2 Cor 5:8). And while this state is no doubt joyous beyond imagination, it is not a permanent place of residence. The apostle John assures the children of God that when Jesus appears they will become like him (1 John 3:2).

Jesus was resurrected in a glorified body and so too will his people be. 1 Corinthians 15:51–53:

> *Behold! I tell you a mystery. We shall not all sleep, but we shall all be changed, in a moment, in the twinkling of an eye, at the last trumpet. For the trumpet will sound, and the dead will be raised*

imperishable, and we shall be changed. For this perishable body must put on the imperishable, and this mortal body must put on immortality.

Those in Christ who have died will be raised with imperishable bodies at his appearing. Then, the still living generation of believers will undergo a magnificent transformation. This change will be from a sinful mortal body into a pure and immortal one. Victory over death and sin is through the Lord Jesus (1 Cor 15:54–57). There is debate among premillennialists as to whether the resurrection of martyred saints during the tribulation happens at the same time as the one mentioned in 1 Corinthians 15:51–53 and 1 Thessalonians 4:16–17. For the purposes here it need only be understood that the resurrection of the just to life (Dan 12:2; Luke 14:14; John 5:29; Rev 20:4) occurs before the Millennium. The rest of the dead are not resurrected until after the Millennium, so that they may face judgment (Rev 20:5, 12).

Those who partake in the resurrection of the just neither marry nor continue in marriage, but are as angels in heaven (Matt 22:30). As a result, the saints in glorified bodies will not produce offspring. Children will, however, continue to be born in the Millennium (Isa 65:20–23; Ezek 47:22). They arise from the second class of millennial residents, those with natural bodies, still mortal, and corrupted by sin (cf. Dan 7:12; Zech 14:16–19). There will be those eager to obey and worship the Lord Jesus while others will be forced to.

GOVERNMENT OFFICIALS

A population consisting of two vastly different groups is to be governed by officials more than equal for the task. Because all the great men and women of faith will have been resurrected, Jesus has an impressive pool from which to draw from in assigning roles. The types of offices and positions in the Millennium vary throughout Scripture. It is unclear as to the specifics of how the offices and branches of government are structured. Only general conclusions can be stated in regard to any sort of hierarchy. What is clear is that all of officials are under the absolute authority of the Monarch.

The King of Kings

Jesus being referred to as the King of kings is well known by many of his followers. A common assumption is that the title is for the purpose of emphasis. It is certainly true that Jesus is a king well above any there ever has been or will be (cf. Ps 95:3). Jesus is also the literal King over other kings because he will destroy those with the power of kings (1 Tim 6:15; Rev 17:12–14). He will strike down the nations and shepherd them with a rod of iron (Ps 2:9; Rev 19:15). It is for this reason that Jesus has the name *King of kings and Lord of lords* written on both his robe and thigh (Rev 19:16). Moreover, Jesus is the Chief Shepherd (1 Pet 5:4) over shepherds after his heart (Jer 3:15). In shepherding the nations, Jesus will oversee many lower level rulers. Several of these individuals are kings in the traditional sense (e.g., Ps 72:10–11), while others are in that they will be given a significant amount of responsibility. Jesus is the King over lower shepherds, rulers, and kings during the Millennium.

Jesus' monarchy is of such necessity that he could not even be the Messiah without it. Isaiah 9:6–7:

> For to us a child is born, to us a son is given; and the government shall be upon his shoulder, and his name shall be called Wonderful Counselor, Mighty God, Everlasting Father, Prince of Peace. Of the increase of his government and of peace there will be no end, on the throne of David and over his kingdom, to establish it and to uphold it with justice and with righteousness from this time forth and forevermore. The zeal of the LORD of hosts will do this.

The Messiah was to arrive as a male baby gifted by God to the Israelites for the purposes of ruling. He was to be wonderful or supernatural in addition to being the perfect counselor and even the Mighty God (v. 6). In many ways these truths were fulfilled by Jesus with his incarnation through a virgin and through his teachings and sacrifice that bring life (Luke 1:31–33; John 1:14; 6:63). In some respects the remaining aspects of this prophecy are in operation now, but they are still working toward a greater realization. The government has not yet been put on Jesus' shoulder in relation to him reigning from David's throne. Once Jesus does occupy this earthly throne he will bear the weight of governance. At present the world is sick with sin. When Jesus fulfills his role as the Son of David, he will uphold his government with justice and righteousness (v. 7; Jer 23:5; 33:15). The LORD promised that the Messiah would bring justice to the nations and not grow faint or be discouraged in doing so (Isa 42:1–4). The increase of peace and dominance of righteousness will begin in the Millennium and continue forever.

The Messiah being referred to as a king is defined by him reigning over all of the earth from Jerusalem. Psalm 2:6–8:

> "As for me, I have set my King on Zion, my holy hill." I will tell of the decree: The LORD said to me, "You are my Son; today I have begotten you. Ask of me, and I will make the nations your heritage, and the ends of the earth your possession.

When King Messiah rules from Jerusalem his authority will not be limited by Israel's borders. Because the Messiah is the Son of God, he inherits control over all the nations. The entirety of the earth is to be Jesus' estate. The King of kings will sit in faithfulness from his throne, established in steadfast love, pursuing justice, and quick to do righteousness (Isa 16:5).

It is of no doubt that Jesus currently rules the Universe from the Father's throne in Heaven (Heb 12:2; Rev 3:21). In the proper context, it is even correct to say that Jesus is currently King of the earth, and he always has been (Jude 1:25). It is for this reason that we must be careful not to confuse passages mandating an earthly rule of Messiah as already being fulfilled.

The necessity of such prophecies being realized only after the Second Coming can be seen in places such as Zechariah 14:9:

> And the LORD will be king over all the earth. On that day the LORD will be one and his name one.

The Messiah will not only be King of the earth, but he is even referred to using God's holy name *YHWH* (translated as *LORD*). The words *on that day* refer to the same day spoken of a few verses earlier in Zechariah 14:4:

> On that day his feet shall stand on the Mount of Olives that lies before Jerusalem on the east, and the Mount of Olives shall be split in two from east to west by a very wide valley, so that one half of the Mount shall move northward, and the other half southward.

This remarkable verse reveals the place where Jesus' feet will first touch the ground at the Second Coming (cf. Acts 1:9–12). It is *on that day* when Jesus returns that he will become King over the earth and establish his government.

Much of what it means for Jesus to be King of kings in the Millennium can be found summarized in Isaiah 24:21–23:

> On that day the LORD will punish the host of heaven, in heaven, and the kings of the earth, on the earth. They will be gathered together as prisoners in a pit; they will be shut up in a prison, and after many days they will be punished. Then the moon will be confounded and the sun ashamed, for the LORD of hosts reigns on Mount Zion and in Jerusalem, and his glory will be before his elders.

The Lord Jesus will demonstrate himself as the only Sovereign by conquering the kings of the earth (v. 21; 1 Tim 6:15; Rev 17:12–14). He will imprison the heavenly host and the kings that opposed him for a period of many days, which is the Millennium (v. 22; Rev 20:2–3). They will then be released, only to face the final punishment (v. 22; Rev 20:7, 10–15). Immeasurable glory is to be found when Jesus reigns from Mount Zion and Jerusalem in the presence of his elders (v. 23).

The crowning of Joshua in Zechariah 6:9–15 is a shadow of the coronation of Jesus at the beginning of his millennial reign. Zechariah 6:12–13:

> And say to him, 'Thus says the LORD of hosts, "Behold, the man whose name is the Branch: for he shall branch out from his place, and he shall build the temple of the LORD. It is he who shall build the temple of the LORD and shall bear royal honor, and shall sit and rule on his throne. And there shall be a priest on his throne, and the counsel of peace shall be between them both."'

The Branch, meaning the King Messiah (cf. Jer 23:5), will build the millennial temple. His consolidated offices of priest and king will be on full display.[1] During his crucifixion, Jesus wore a crown of thorns (e.g., Matt 27:29). During his millennial reign, Jesus will wear an ornate crown of silver and gold (Zech 6:11).

The Prince Over Israel

In the latter days the children of Israel will seek the LORD and David their king (Hos 3:5). The Israelites will serve the LORD and David, whom will be raised up for their sake (Jer 30:9). David's position will be of such

---

1. See Psalm 110 and Hebrews 7 for more on the Messiah being both a priest and a king like Melchizedek.

prominence in Israel that only King Jesus will hold a higher office. Ezekiel 34:23–24:

> And I will set up over them one shepherd, my servant David, and he shall feed them: he shall feed them and be their shepherd. And I, the LORD, will be their God, and my servant David shall be prince among them. I am the LORD; I have spoken.

The LORD promised to rescue his flock Israel and judge between the sheep (Ezek 34:22). After he does so, Jesus will install David as the shepherd who will feed Israel (v. 23). This is not unlike Jesus assigning Peter as a shepherd who was to feed the sheep that are God's people (John 21:15–17). While David is to be the prince over Israel, he will always remain a subject of the LORD Jesus (v. 24). This may be why David is spoken of as a prince in some passages and as a king in others. David will be a king relative to Israel but only a prince when compared to the King of kings. In Ezekiel 37:24–25, David is referred to as being both a king and a prince in the same narrative. The use of both titles hints at David's status as the head of Israel while he serves under the Sovereign of the entire earth.

Prince David's duties will include collecting and then presenting sacrifices on behalf of the people of Israel (Ezek 45:16–17; 46:4–12). He will eat from these sacrificial meals before the Lord Jesus in the hallowed outer east gate of the temple (Ezek 44:1–3; 46:12). David will enjoy the privilege of overseeing the observance of the Passover and the Feast of Tabernacles. On Passover, the prince will provide for the people and himself a bull for a sin offering. He shall present various other offerings during the seven days of Passover and the seven days of the Feast of Tabernacles (Ezek 45:21–25).

The prestige attached to David in these passages has led even those who usually interpret the Bible literally to argue that it is actually the Messiah who is in mind here. The claim is that Jesus was referred to as David because the Messiah comes from his line. This is impossible. Jesus would never need to provide a sin offering for himself, nor does he have sons (Ezek 46:16). The Messiah is divine (e.g., Isa 9:6–7); it is he who is called LORD in Ezekiel 44:1–3. In this passage and others the LORD is differentiated from Ezekiel's prince. Even if the prince mentioned in Ezekiel chapters 44–46 was distinct from David the prince in Ezekiel chapters 34 and 37, there is still nothing in those contexts that identifies *David* as the Messiah. Also, none of the passages refer to the *Son* or *Branch of David*, which is what one would expect when the Messiah is the subject. Even if the Messiah is to fulfill some of these prophecies, David will undoubtedly occupy a high office. It is perfectly in keeping with the overall thrust of Scripture that David would be given much responsibility in the Millennial Kingdom. David is mentioned almost a thousand times in God's word. The only man mentioned or referred to more often is Jesus himself.

The Heads of the Twelve Tribes

The number twelve is often used in the Bible to signify perfection of governance. Examples include twelve months in a year, twelve hours in a day (John 11:9), twelve pillars erected at Mt. Sinai (Exod 24:4), twelve stones taken from the Jordan that were set up in Gilgal (Josh 4), twelve Hebrews selected to conduct the census (Num 1:2–16), twelve legions of angels (Matt 26:53), and twelve types of fruit on the Tree of Life (Rev 22:2).[2] When Jesus chose apostles to make up his inner circle, it was no accident that there were twelve. That number alone tells us that on some level the twelve represent the tribes of Israel. This representation was not limited to the period of the First Coming until each of the twelve died. In electing the twelve, Jesus had their future positions in mind. Matthew 19:28:

> Jesus said to them, "Truly, I say to you, in the new world, when the Son of Man will sit on his glorious throne, you who have followed me will also sit on twelve thrones, judging the twelve tribes of Israel.

Jesus spoke of a new world marked by him sitting upon his glorious throne. Those twelve of Jesus' closest followers will sit upon their own thrones as judges over the tribes of Israel. It is likely that these twelve thrones will be in close proximity to Jesus' own Davidic throne. Just as Jesus sat down next to Father's throne in Heaven, so too will overcomers sit down next to Jesus' throne (Rev 3:21). Due to the numerical matching, each of the twelve will likely have his own tribe to manage. Think of the twelve as department heads in the overall government of Israel.

A synoptic account is recorded in Luke 22:28–30:

> "You are those who have stayed with me in my trials, and I assign to you, as my Father assigned to me, a kingdom, that you may eat and drink at my table in my kingdom and sit on thrones judging the twelve tribes of Israel.

---

2. More examples include Gen 49:28; 1 Kgs 7:25; Num 7:10–83, 13:1–15; Luke 2:41; Matt 10:2–4; Rev 7:4; 21:12; and 21:16–17.

Not only will the twelve sit on thrones next to Jesus, but they will also have seats at his table. The imagery of eating together emphasizes the intimacy that the twelve will have with the King. It is thought of as desirable to have the ear of an influential person. This is the greatest example of that level of access. Jesus vowed that he would not drink wine again until he could do it with the twelve in the coming kingdom (Matt 26:29). The twelve will have the privilege of eating and drinking with the King of kings on a regular basis.

Eleven of the heads over the tribes are identified as Simon Peter, Andrew, James the son of Zebedee, John his brother, Philip, Bartholomew, Thomas, Matthew, James the son of Alphaeus, Thaddeus, and Simon the Zealot (Matt 10:2–4). Judas will not be joining his former colleagues, for he is in his own place, separated from God (Acts 1:25). The final head of the tribes will either be Matthias or Paul. Matthias is unique in that he was the only member of the twelve not directly chosen by Jesus (Acts 1:26). Paul was directly chosen by Jesus to be his apostle (Acts 9:1–18; 26:12–18; Rom 1:1). It is for this reason that many speculate that it was Paul who was the actual replacement for Judas. A position is not taken here, but the possibility needs to be acknowledged. Regardless, both Matthias and Paul are going to occupy high offices in the Millennium.

The Signet Ring

Zerubbabel led the first group of Israelites back from the Babylonian captivity (Ezra 2:1–2), constructed the second temple (Ezra 5:2), and is in the direct line of ancestry to Jesus, possibly serving as a common link to both Joseph (Matt 1:12) and Mary (Luke 3:27). As a reward for his service, the LORD bestowed a special honor upon Zerubbabel in Haggai 2:23:

> On that day, declares the LORD of hosts, I will take you, O Zerubbabel my servant, the son of Shealtiel, declares the LORD, and make you like a signet ring, for I have chosen you, declares the LORD of hosts."

This prophecy will come to pass *on that day*. This refers to the time identified in the previous verse, when the LORD will overthrow the thrones and kingdoms of man (Hag 2:22), and replace them with the throne and kingdom of Jesus (Dan 2:44). Zerubbabel being made a signet ring means that he will represent a dignitary in much the same way that a flag or standard bearer does. On many levels Zerubbabel already serves as a type pointing to Jesus. Jesus too will reestablish his people in the Promised Land and build a vastly superior temple (Zech 6:12–13). In the Millennium, it will be Zerubbabel's official role to make people look to and think of Jesus.

Restored Judges

The offices of judge and counselor will be reinstituted. Isaiah 1:26:

> And I will restore your judges as at the first, and your counselors as at the beginning. Afterward you shall be called the city of righteousness, the faithful city."

Not only will there be judges active in Israel but they will even function as they were originally intended to. Their guidance is a step toward Jerusalem becoming a righteous and faithful city. Because so many of the other offices are occupied by resurrected saints, in all likelihood this will be the case with some of the judges as well. Great judges from Israel's past such as Othniel, Gideon, and the mighty Samson will once again exercise authority in Israel.

God's Princes

David will not be the only one to occupy the office of prince. Though their duties are less specific, there will be a plurality of princes ruling in justice under King Jesus (Isa 32:1). Ezekiel 45:8:

> of the land. It is to be his property in Israel. And my princes shall no more oppress my people, but they shall let the house of Israel have the land according to their tribes.

God referred to his own princes. These men are set in contradistinction to the violent and oppressive princes of Israel in Ezekiel's time (Ezek 45:9). Part of the princes' duties will be to ensure that each tribe has its rightful portion of land. Because of this, it is possible that these princes are the twelve disciples because they are to be the heads of the twelve tribes (Matt 19:28). Regardless, there will be several prolific saints living in the Millennium that do not have a specific office mentioned. They are, then, princes in a generic sense even if they will not hold that title.

Abraham is one of these great saints. He is the father to all of those who have been saved through faith in Jesus (Gal 3:7). He serves as the foremost example of a sinner being counted as righteous for trusting in God (Gen 15:6; Rom 4:1–5). Abraham was called a friend of God by the LORD and others (2 Chr 20:7; Isa 41:8; Jas 2:23). The blessings found in the Millennium are based on the unconditional covenants. And these covenants are all rooted in the promises made by God to Abraham. Abraham is our father in the faith, a friend of God, and will be a prince in the Millennium.

Isaac and Jacob are critical patriarchs; their notoriety will remain throughout eternity. The blessing to Abraham was transferred through Isaac (Gen 26:12; 26:3–4) and his son Jacob (Gen 28:14–15) to the twelve tribes (Gen 49:1–28). Isaac and Jacob are of such importance that, at times, the Creator of the universe referred to himself as the God of Abraham, Isaac, and Jacob (e.g., Exod 3:6). We can glean some of Jacob's future importance from the blessing Isaac bestowed upon him in Genesis 27:27–29:

> So he came near and kissed him. And Isaac smelled the smell of his garments and blessed him and said, "See, the smell of my son is as the smell of a field that the Lord has blessed! May God give you of the dew of heaven and of the fatness of the earth and plenty of grain and wine. Let peoples serve you, and nations bow down to you. Be lord over your brothers, and may your mother's sons bow down to you. Cursed be everyone who curses you, and blessed be everyone who blesses you!"

The blessing made to Jacob applies to his descendants as a whole. However, Jacob is the immediate recipient of this blessing and it is to him that primary application must be assigned. Jacob died without ever receiving the fatness of the earth and a great abundance of food. On the contrary, Jacob had to send his sons to Egypt to buy grain on account of famine in the land (Gen 42:1–5; 3:1–2). The nations never served or bowed before Jacob. Instead, he served Laban for twenty years (Gen 31:41) and even bowed before Esau (Gen 33:3). The Millennium allows for Isaac's blessing to be realized. This signals that Jacob will be a prince along with his father Isaac.

Job demonstrated great faith that he would be resurrected in Job 19:25–26:

> For I know that my Redeemer lives, and at the last he will stand upon the earth. And after my skin has been thus destroyed, yet in my flesh I shall see God,

Job is well known for being a man of righteousness because he trusted in the LORD. Part of that trust included an understanding that Job's Redeemer was God himself. And even though Job's body would rot away, he knew that he would once again live in his flesh and witness the Messiah standing upon the earth in the last days. A man so confident in the resurrection will probably play an important role in the subsequent government. This reasoning extends to any who were similar in their righteousness, including Noah and Daniel (Ezek 14:20). Further candidates include anyone of great faith, such as those listed in the Hebrews hall of faith (Heb 11).

The Body of Christ

The book of Hebrews opens with a formal oration on the supremacy of the Son of God (Heb 1:1–4). Then, in various ways the Son's superiority is proven by demonstrating that he is greater than the angels (Heb 1:5–13; 2:5). This indicates just how exalted of a station the angels enjoy. Jesus was temporarily of a lower position than the angels when he took on flesh (Heb 2:9). In the order of creation, man is on a rung below that of the angels (Heb 2:7)

This recognition provides the proper backdrop by which to fully appreciate the role of the Body of Christ in the Millennium. 1 Corinthians 6:2–3:

> Or do you not know that the saints will judge the world? And if the world is to be judged by you, are you incompetent to try trivial cases? Do you not know that we are to judge angels? How much more, then, matters pertaining to this life!

The members of the Body will be conformed to the image of Jesus (Rom 8:29; 2 Cor 3:18), being made like him (1 John 3:2). The extent to which the saints are to be like Jesus is debatable. What is clear is that the level of improvement will be enough to place them above the angels. Not only will the Body of Christ judge the world of men, but even that of the angels.

Reigning Saints

The rule of saints under Jesus is explicitly said to occur during the Millennium in Revelation 20:4–6:

> Then I saw thrones, and seated on them were those to whom the authority to judge was committed. Also I saw the souls of those who had been beheaded for the testimony of Jesus and for the word of

God, and those who had not worshiped the beast or its image and had not received its mark on their foreheads or their hands. They came to life and reigned with Christ for a thousand years. The rest of the dead did not come to life until the thousand years were ended. This is the first resurrection. Blessed and holy is the one who shares in the first resurrection! Over such the second death has no power, but they will be priests of God and of Christ, and they will reign with him for a thousand years.

The people sitting on the thrones might be a reference to the twelve only (v. 4). It may also include all believers that were granted such an honor at the Judgment Seat of Christ (2 Cor 5:10). The saints who refused to take the mark of the beast and were martyred for the testimony of Jesus are to be resurrected and given authority (v. 4). These tribulation saints are mentioned separately, implying that they have a unique position in the government. The remaining deceased are not resurrected until after the Millennium (v. 5), and this is to face judgment and damnation (v. 6; Rev 20:12–15). All of the saints throughout history will have been resurrected and will have received their glorified bodies by the end of the Millennium. They are blessed and holy because they have eternal life through faith in Jesus. The blood of Jesus has been applied to those in the first resurrection (Rom 3:25), empowering them to share in his reign (v. 6).

Previously, the apostle John provided us with a point of clarification in Revelation 5:9–10:

And they sang a new song, saying, "Worthy are you to take the scroll and to open its seals, for you were slain, and by your blood you ransomed people for God from every tribe and language and people and nation, and you have made them a kingdom and priests to our God, and they shall reign on the earth."

The reigning saints include every single person ransomed by the blood of Jesus, regardless of ethnicity (v. 9). That means that no saved person will be left out or remain in Heaven during the Millennium. All of God's people will become a kingdom of priests, reigning alongside Jesus, here on the earth (v. 10; cf. Isa 66:21). The greatness of the world's kingdoms shall be given to the people of the saints of the Most High (Dan 7:27).

John did not spill much ink in covering the Millennium in his apocalypse. The reign of the saints with Christ being one of the few points mentioned highlights its importance. All of those as of yet unfulfilled passages about various men and women obtaining great authority in the kingdom find their home here.

THE BEMA SEAT OF CHRIST

Those who never came to have a saving knowledge of Jesus will face judgment before the Great White Throne. Because the unsaved do not have the blood of the Lamb to cover their sins (Rom 3:25), God will judge them based on their works, find them guilty, and then throw them into the lake of fire (Rev 20:11–15). This is a radically different judgment than the one where believers will stand before God to give an account (Rom 14:10–12). The judgment of the saints is not to determine one's final fate, for that was decided for each believer the second he or she came to trust in the work and person of Jesus Christ (e.g., John 3:16; Rom 8:1). Paul explicitly stated that even those with perishable works will be saved (1 Cor 3:15).

This judgment will be for the purpose of rewarding the servants, prophets, saints, and those who fear God's name (Rev 11:18). These awards determine one's office in the Millennial Kingdom. 2 Corinthians 5:10:

> For we must all appear before the judgment seat of Christ, so that each one may receive what is due for what he has done in the body, whether good or evil.

This will be a time for regret, as those who love Jesus will face their own sin and failings in serving him. The greater emphasis, though, will be on believers being honored for their faith and obedience. It is the very Greek word *bema*, translated here as *judgment*, that indicates an awards ceremony. The imagery of this judgment comes from the ancient Olympic Games, where from a raised structure a judge would determine how athletes performed and what crowns they were to be awarded.

The most telling passage on how to perform well at the bema seat of Christ is found in 1 Corinthians 3:10–15:

> According to the grace of God given to me, like a skilled master builder I laid a foundation, and someone else is building upon it. Let each one take care how he builds upon it. For no one can lay a foundation other than that which is laid, which is Jesus Christ. Now if anyone builds on the foundation with gold, silver, precious stones, wood, hay, straw—each one's work will become manifest, for the Day will disclose it, because it will be revealed by fire, and the fire will test what sort of work each one has done. If the work

that anyone has built on the foundation survives, he will receive a reward. If anyone›s work is burned up, he will suffer loss, though he himself will be saved, but only as through fire.

Those who build upon the foundation that is Jesus Christ (v. 11) must be careful to use works that are enduring like gold, silver, and precious stones. And not those that are perishable like wood, hay, and straw (v. 12). At the judgment, fire will burn away all the combustible works and leave only those that were truly done for the sake of Christ (v. 13). The works that survive the testing flames will determine one's level of reward (v. 14). The works that are burned up are those that were not done according to God's will. These incinerated works indicate a loss of reward (v. 15), for they will ultimately add up to nothing but ash.

Crowns

Though there may be several more, Scripture tells us that there are at least five different crowns that the saints are eligible to earn by running the race well (2 Tim 2:5; Heb 12:1). These awards also borrow from the ancient Olympics, where athletes were crowned with laurel wreaths to signify performance. The first of these prizes is the *imperishable crown*. This will be awarded to those saints who denied themselves and brought their old natures into subjugation (1 Cor 9:25). Athletes practice self-control in order to obtain the perishable wreath. The honor that comes from God remains forever.

The *crown of boasting* is earned by soul winners. It will be worn by those evangelists who took joy in being used to bring others to the Lord (1 Thess 2:19–20). Those who turn many to righteousness will shine like the stars forever (Dan 12:3). The *crown of righteousness* is to be expected by all those who have loved his appearing (2 Tim 4:7–8). The return of Jesus is often mocked or minimalized, not only by unbelievers, but even by some who claim to know him. In contrast, the truth of his coming is so important to Jesus that he will reward those who longed for the blessed hope (Titus 2:13).

God has promised the *crown of life* to those that love him and have remained steadfast under trial (Jas 1:12). This especially includes those who are tested to the point of martyrdom (Rev 2:10). The final crown is the unfading *crown of glory*. It will be awarded to those shepherds or church leaders that served and discipled their flocks without lording over them (1

Pet 5:1–4). It may seem unfair that this crown is apparently only available to church leaders. Some balance comes in that those who become teachers will be held to stricter standards (Jas 3:1).

Though the crowns and other awards are significant in the kingdom, the greatest joy in earning them will be in casting them at Jesus' feet (Rev 4:10–11). Even though the faithful rightly earned their rewards, the ability to do so came from abiding in Jesus. Apart from him, the Christian could not produce any genuine fruit (John 15:5). Those great in the Millennium will have the opportunity to worship Jesus by attributing all that they are back to him.

Greatest in the Kingdom

The conclusion that the awards issued by Christ indicate one's office in the Millennium is inferred from several passages that speak of being great or not so great in the coming kingdom. The principles derived from these many passages are simple. To humble yourself like a child in the present world is to become great in the coming one (Matt 18:1–4). Those who are first will be last, and the last will be first (Matt 19:30). The meek are to inherit the earth (Matt 5:5). The meek will not just be living upon the earth, but they will enjoy authority under Christ in reigning over it.

MANDATORY WORSHIP

Whether they are saved or not, all people will recognize the divinity and kingship of Jesus (Zech 14:9). Every knee shall bow and every tongue will swear allegiance to the LORD God (Isa 45:23; Rom 14:11). Paul both clarified and elaborated on this prophecy from Isaiah by writing that at the name of Jesus every knee shall bow and every tongue will confess that Jesus Christ is Lord. This includes people in Heaven, Hell, and notably those on the earth (Phil 2:10). Indeed, the very reason that Jesus is given dominion and a kingdom is so that all peoples, nations, and languages should serve him (Dan 7:14). The role of the kingdom's government is to oversee the service owed to the Messiah and to ensure that it is according to his desired order.

All types of people, ranging from nomads to kings, will travel in order to bow before Jesus. This was foreseen by Solomon in Psalm 72:8–11:

May he have dominion from sea to sea, and from the River to the ends of the earth! May desert tribes bow down before him, and his enemies lick the dust! May the kings of Tarshish and of the coast-lands render him tribute; may the kings of Sheba and Seba bring gifts! May all kings fall down before him, all nations serve him!

The Messiah is to rule over the entire earth (v. 8); his enemies will suffer total defeat (v. 9). Tarshish is probably located in modern-day Spain, while Sheba is Yemen and Seba is Sudan. The kings and peoples of all the nations will bring gifts, including gold and frankincense, to set before King Jesus (v. 10; Isa 60:6, 9, 11). The nations that refuse to serve Israel and her Messiah will perish and be utterly ruined (Isa 60:12). The point is that rulers from diverse places around the world will all come to pay tribute to he who holds true authority. Wise men traveled from the east to worship the child Jesus (Matt 2:1–2) and to bring him gifts of gold, frankincense, and myrrh (Matt 2:11). This was a preview of what will happen on a global scale when wise men, and not-so-wise men, will submit to the authority of the Messiah.

While some will joyfully choose to worship Jesus, others will be forced to bend the knee. Zechariah 14:16–17:

Then everyone who survives of all the nations that have come against Jerusalem shall go up year after year to worship the King, the LORD of hosts, and to keep the Feast of Booths. And if any of the families of the earth do not go up to Jerusalem to worship the King, the LORD of hosts, there will be no rain on them.

After the Second Coming, survivors from the nations that opposed Jerusalem and sought to murder the Jewish remnant will have to travel to the city annually to worship Jesus and observe the Feast of Tabernacles. This requirement is extended to all of the families of the earth. If representatives from nations and families do not travel to worship Jesus then rain will be withheld from their land. Egypt is mentioned as an example, with the absence of rain described as a kind of plague (Zech 14:18). In teaching on the importance of loving your enemies, Jesus pointed out that God sends rain on both the just and unjust (Matt 5:45). During the Millennium, if people do not come to humble themselves before the Messiah, then even this common grace will no longer be taken for granted.

6

Jerusalem: Capital of the World

LET US GO WITH YOU

FAMILIES FROM ALL THE earth will be making pilgrimages to Jerusalem to worship Jesus, for he will be ruling from the capital of the world. Zechariah 8:20–23:

> *"Thus says the LORD of hosts: Peoples shall yet come, even the inhabitants of many cities. The inhabitants of one city shall go to another, saying, 'Let us go at once to entreat the favor of the LORD and to seek the LORD of hosts; I myself am going.' Many peoples and strong nations shall come to seek the LORD of hosts in Jerusalem and to entreat the favor of the LORD. Thus says the LORD of hosts: In those days ten men from the nations of every tongue shall take hold of the robe of a Jew, saying, 'Let us go with you, for we have heard that God is with you.'"*

Gentiles from around the globe will be excited to travel to Jerusalem to beseech the Lord Jesus. This includes those nations that are more powerful than the others (vv. 20–21). Here is a beautiful picture of the Jews finally becoming the head and not the tail among the nations (Deut 28:13). Many sick people touched the fringe on Jesus' garment and were made well through their faith (Matt 9:20–22; 14:35–36). Out of the same desire for a blessing, people from all nations will take hold of the corner of a Jew's garment and be led to Jesus. All of the peoples of the earth will recognize that the Jews are called by the name of the LORD and shall be in awe of them (v.

23; Deut 28:10). The opportunity to latch onto a Jew will be common place. Jew and Gentile will regularly travel to the mountain height of Israel, for it is where all of them shall serve the LORD (cf. Isa 56:7; Ezek 20:40).

The Holy Highway

Travel to Jerusalem will be so routine that a special highway for pilgrims will run through Israel. The highway will be called the *Way of Holiness*, because only the redeemed will be permitted to travel on it and even fools will not lose their way (Isa 35:8–9). No dangerous animals will be present on the highway and sorrow will flee from the travelers (Isa 35:9). The pilgrims will be filled with everlasting joy as they sing on their way to Zion (Isa 35:10).

The highway will also connect Israel to her neighbors. Isaiah 19:23–24:

> In that day there will be a highway from Egypt to Assyria, and As-syria will come into Egypt, and Egypt into Assyria, and the Egyp-tians will worship with the Assyrians. In that day Israel will be the third of Egypt and Assyria, a blessing in the midst of the earth,

The highway will begin in Egypt, run through Jerusalem and the Arabah, and end in Assyria (northeast of Israel) (v. 23; Isa 35:6–10). This will allow the Egyptians and Assyrians to journey to each other's countries and to worship with one another. This will be made possible by the blessing of Israel binding the nations together. The Egyptians and Assyrians will be able to travel from their respective ends of the highway to Zion for worship (Isa 35:10). This astounding highway is part of God's plan in making Egypt his people and Assyria the work of his hands (Isa 19:25). The three countries being united essentially cover the land that was promised to Abram's descendants (Gen 15:18).

GO UP TO JERUSALEM

People are said to go *up to* Jerusalem when traveling there regardless of whether they are actually traveling north or increasing in elevation (e.g., Ezra 1:3). Jerusalem is spiritually the highest place on earth. This is in anticipation of the millennial Jerusalem, when the city will literally be the highest place on earth. This uplifted mountain symbolizes the center of the world's government and worship in several places, including Isaiah 2:2–4:

It shall come to pass in the latter days that the mountain of the house of the LORD shall be established as the highest of the mountains, and shall be lifted up above the hills; and all the nations shall flow to it, and many peoples shall come, and say: "Come, let us go up to the mountain of the LORD, to the house of the God of Jacob, that he may teach us his ways and that we may walk in his paths." For out of Zion shall go the law, and the word of the LORD from Jerusalem. He shall judge between the nations, and decide disputes for many peoples; and they shall beat their swords into plowshares, and their spears into pruning hooks; nation shall not lift up sword against other nation, neither shall they learn war anymore.

Pilgrimages to Jerusalem are to become so dense that it will appear as if the nations of the world are flowing toward the mountain like water (v. 2; Mic 4:1). Numerous people will travel to the mountain because it is where they shall receive instruction from the LORD and become his followers (v. 3; Mic 4:2). Think of this as the Great Commission in reverse. It is atop this mountain where Jesus will be the supreme judge, settling disputes between distant countries, and determining the course for many peoples. Under the Messiah's governance, nations will finally be at perfect peace with one another (v. 4; Mic 4:3).

Some may object to the literal fulfilment of the Isaiah and Micah passages, and those related to them, based on John 4:20–24. There, Jesus told a Samaritan woman that the hour was coming when neither on Mount Gerizim nor in Jerusalem will the Father be worshipped (v. 21). But the point of Jesus' teaching was not to preclude any future worship in Jerusalem at all. Rather, because God is spirit, true worshippers will worship him in spirit and truth (vv. 23–24). Jesus did not choose to become mired in the debate between the Samaritans and the Jews on where legitimate worship was to be had. Instead, he emphasized what true worship was. When Jesus reigns from Jerusalem, the fact will remain that God can only be genuinely worshipped by those who do so in spirit and truth, regardless of their location.

The Coronation Banquet

Something special that the saints may look forward to on top of the mountain is found in Isaiah 25:6:

On this mountain the LORD of hosts will make for all peoples a feast of rich food, a feast of well-aged wine, of rich food full of marrow, of aged wine well refined.

Observing the crowning of a king of Israel with a feast was a common practice (e.g., 1 Sam 11:15; 1 Kgs 1:9, 19, 25). At David's inauguration he distributed various foods to the whole multitude of Israel (2 Sam 6:17–19). Solomon too held a feast for all Israel, sacrificing 22,000 oxen and 120,000 sheep to the LORD (1 Kgs 8:62–65). After his coronation at the beginning of the Millennium, Jesus is going to prepare a lavish banquet! People will come to the height of Zion shouting for joy, beaming over the bounty of the LORD. Grain, wine, and choice meats will be enjoyed along with dancing. God will fill the souls of the priests, and his people will be satisfied with his goodness (Jer 31:12–14). Many will come from east and west to recline at the same table with Abraham, Isaac, and Jacob (Matt 8:11). A shadow of this feast occurred when Moses, Aaron, Nadab, Abihu, and seventy of Israel's elders went part way up Mount Sinai, beholding God as they ate and drank (Exod 24:9–11). Enjoying a meal with your Creator will be an important part of worship.

Ezekiel's Tour

In a vision, Ezekiel was taken on a royal tour of the mountain's summit. He first beheld that on the south side was a city, the millennial Jerusalem (Ezek 40:2–3; cf. Zech 2:1–2). Ezekiel was then shown extensive details regarding the millennial temple that also sits atop the mountain (Ezek 40–44). Specifics on how the summit of the mountain is to be measured and divided are provided in Ezekiel 45:1–7:

"When you allot the land as an inheritance, you shall set apart for the LORD a portion of the land as a holy district, 25,000 cubits long and 20,000 cubits broad. It shall be holy throughout its whole extent. Of this a square plot of 500 by 500 cubits shall be for the sanctuary, with fifty cubits for an open space around it. And from this measured district you shall measure off a section 25,000 cubits long and 10,000 broad, in which shall be the sanctuary, the Most Holy Place. It shall be the holy portion of the land. It shall be for the priests, who minister in the sanctuary and approach the LORD to minister to him, and it shall be a place for their houses and a holy place for the sanctuary. Another section, 25,000 cubits long and 10,000 cubits broad, shall be for the Levites who minister at the temple, as their

possession for cities to live in. "Alongside the portion set apart as the holy district you shall assign for the property of the city an area 5,000 cubits broad and 25,000 cubits long. It shall belong to the whole house of Israel. "And to the prince shall belong the land on both sides of the holy district and the property of the city, alongside the holy district and the property of the city, on the west and on the east, corresponding in length to one of the tribal portions, and extending from the western to the eastern boundary

Unfortunately most modern translations, including the one used in this book, indicate that the all the measurements, on and of the summit, were made in cubits. The Hebrew does not provide any word for the unit of measurement in the passage. This is because the prophet already told us that the measurements were done in reeds, which are the equivalent of six long cubits each (Ezek 40:5). Measured in reeds, the summit's plateau is almost fifty miles in length and width (v. 1; Ezek 48:8). The summit is holy throughout because it will be a home to both the Lord Jesus and the messianic temple (vv. 1–3). The temple will measure about one square mile (v. 2). The designated area for the temple and the sons of Zadok priests will be nearly fifty miles in length and twenty miles in width (vv. 3–4; Ezek 48:10–11). The Levites will have their own area, also measuring fifty by twenty miles. They will be unable to trade or sell it, for the land is holy to the LORD (v. 5; Ezek 48:13). Jerusalem is to sit in the middle of her own property of fifty miles long by ten miles wide. The city will be surrounded by open country for common use and for the housing of all the tribes of Israel (v. 6; Ezek 48:15–19). Prince David shall own the land on both sides of Jerusalem's property and the holy district. These farmlands will be tilled by all the tribes of Israel, providing food for the workers of Jerusalem (v. 7; Ezek 48:18–19).

THE MILLENNIAL JERUSALEM

The LORD declared that the days are coming when Jerusalem is to be rebuilt from corner to corner (Jer 31:38–39). The first thing we should recognize about the millennial Jerusalem is that she is entirely holy. Just as in Jeremiah's day, the infamous valley of Ben-Hinnom now lies to the west and south of the city. This is where some Israelites worshipped Canaanite gods like Baal and Molech by sacrificing their children in fire. This practice was so depraved that it never even entered the LORD's mind. As a result, the valley was cursed and God renamed it the Valley of Slaughter (Jer 7:31–32; 19:2–6). The valley is referred to as *Gehenna* in the New Testament and was mentioned by Jesus eleven times as an earthly representation of the suffering found in unquenchable hellfire (e.g., Matt 10:28; Mark 9:43). In stark contrast, this once accursed and unclean valley shall become sacred to the LORD, including its very ashes (Jer 31:40). The other major valley outside of Jerusalem, the Kidron, and to the corner of the Horse Gate toward the east, will be holy to the LORD. The city and her territory will never be invaded or taken again (Jer 31:40).

Within Jerusalem, objects as minor as the bells on horses will be inscribed with *Holy to the LORD* (Zech 14:20). This is precisely what was written upon the plate of pure gold worn by Aaron the high priest on his turban (Exod 28:36–38). What was once intended for the high priest will now be written upon some of the most common items. Every pot in Jerusalem and Judah will be holy to the degree that they are likened to the bowls used before the altar (Zech 14:21). The distinction between the secular and the sacred will be no more in the great city.

The millennial Jerusalem measures ten miles by ten miles square (Ezek 48:16, 35). She is to have twelve gates, three on each side, each named after a tribe of Israel (Ezek 48:30–34). The primary purpose of these gates is revealed in Isaiah 60:11–12:

> Your gates shall be open continually; day and night they shall not be shut, that people may bring to you the wealth of the nations, with their kings led in procession. For the nation and kingdom that will not serve you shall perish; those nations shall be utterly laid waste.

The gates must remain open so that the kings of the nations can bring their tributes to the people of Jerusalem. Vast caravans of treasure-bearing camels will cover the land of Israel. The Gentiles on their backs will proclaim the praises of the LORD (Isa 60:6). This is part of what it means for the nations of the earth to submit to King Jesus. Remember that kings and tribes are to come lick the dust and bow before the feet of the Messiah (Ps 72:9). Likewise, kings, queens, and other descendants of those who once hated and afflicted the people of Jerusalem will come to bow at their feet, licking the dust. They will call Jerusalem *the City of the LORD, the Zion of the Holy One of Israel* (Isa 49:23; 60:14). Once the Jews were forced to build cities in Egypt (Exod 1:11). In a stunning reversal, it is foreigners who will build and maintain the very walls of Jerusalem (Isa 60:10). The service rendered by the nations is one of the methods God will use to transform the city from being hated into a joy lasting forever (Isa 60:15). Jerusalem sucking the milk of nations and the breast of kings is also how Jesus, the divine Savior and the Mighty One of Jacob, reminds the city's inhabitants of who he is (Isa 60:16).

A Spreading Metropolis

Zechariah was given a vision that encouraged the rebuilding of Jerusalem in his day, but was ultimately looking forward to the Millennium. Zechariah 2:1–5:

> And I lifted my eyes and saw, and behold, a man with a measuring line in his hand! Then I said, "Where are you going?" And he said to me, "To measure Jerusalem, to see what is its width and what is its length." And behold, the angel who talked with me came forward, and another angel came forward to meet him and said to him, "Run, say to that young man, 'Jerusalem shall be inhabited as villages without walls, because of the multitude of people and livestock in it. And I will be to her a wall of fire all around, declares the LORD, and I will be the glory in her midst.'"

Like with Ezekiel, Zechariah is visited by an angel with a measuring line in his hand, showing the prophet the future dimensions and glory of Jerusalem (vv. 1–2). During the restoration following the Babylonian exile, walls were built around the city so that the people would feel safe. However, most Jews were so afraid of living in Jerusalem that they cast lots, resulting in only a tenth of them moving there. Those who were actually willing to live in Jerusalem were blessed by the people (Neh 11:1–2). Jerusalem became wide and large but there were few inhabitants and no rebuilt houses (Neh 7:4). This is not the picture we see here, where Jerusalem is to be as a city without walls due to the overflowing number of inhabitants and livestock; a place where houses, fields, and vineyards shall be purchased (vv. 3–4; Jer 32:15). While this vision encouraged the rebuilding of Jerusalem, that effort did not fulfill it. The LORD protecting Jerusalem as a wall of fire harkens back to him as the guardian pillar of fire (e.g., Exod 13:21–22; Isa 4:5–6). When the Lord Messiah in your midst, no walls are needed.

The LORD is There

At this time, Jerusalem will be called by a new name: *The LORD is there* (Ezek 48:35). The Hebrew for this compound name, *YHWH-shammah*, only appears once in the entire Tanakh. It is descriptive of when much of God's design and desire to dwell in Jerusalem forever will be realized (cf. Ps 132:13–14). The city's rebuilding is specifically for the LORD (Jer 31:38). David is to always have a lamp before the LORD in Jerusalem, for it is the city where he has chosen to put his name forever (1 Kgs 11:36; 1 Chr 33:4). In the Sermon on the Mount, Jesus taught against making oaths by Jerusalem, for it is the city of the great king, meaning Jesus himself (Matt 5:35; cf. Ps 48:2). This is why both the Messiah and Jerusalem will be called *the LORD is our righteousness* (Jer 23:6; 33:16).

Ezekiel opened his book with a vision of a storm, picturing the coming judgment upon Jerusalem (Ezek 1:4). The prophet went on to behold the departure of the Glory of the LORD from the temple in Jerusalem (Ezek 10:18–19; 11:22–23). As sorrowful as these visions were, at the conclusion of his book, Ezekiel was blessed to witness the city exalted, the LORD having returned there permanently. The name YHWH-shammah is both unique and incredibly comforting, for it describes Jerusalem when the Lord Jesus will be there.

7

The Messianic Millennial Temple

THE BOOK OF EZEKIEL's final nine chapters are among the most fascinating in all of Scripture. Despite this, they are all too often ignored by the majority of Christians. One of the reasons being that many students of Scripture simply do not know what to make of what they are reading. For the chapters describe an astonishing temple, producing wonders, that has not yet come into existence. Additionally, the temple is used for animal sacrifices; something that has apparently been done away with. However, Ezekiel is surely a true prophet and thus his prophecies must come to pass in every detail just as described (cf. Deut 18:20–22). Therefore, we can be assured that a new temple is yet to be built, matching the one foreseen by the prophet. It will not be constructed until after Jesus returns to set up his kingdom. And yet, there will be no temple in the Eternal State (Rev 21:22). We can then rightly infer that Ezekiel's temple is a messianic millennial temple.

MESSIAH'S HOUSE

While the details of this temple are in his final chapters, the prophet previously foretold of its arrival in Ezekiel 37:26–28:

> I will make a covenant of peace with them. It shall be an everlasting covenant with them. And I will set them in their land and multiply them, and will set my sanctuary in their midst forevermore. My dwelling place shall be with them, and I will be their God, and they shall be my people. Then the nations will know that I am the LORD who sanctifies Israel, when my sanctuary is in their midst forevermore.

Once Israel is brought into the New Covenant she will be in an obedient relationship with God, dwelling safely with him in the Promised Land (v. 26). This allows for the ideal temple to finally arise, for the LORD requires his own house (vv. 26–27). Among all the reasons in the Millennium for the nations to be aware of the fact that the God of Israel is the LORD, the temple is specifically mentioned as a cause (v. 28).

Her Construction

One of the reasons for the nations' keen awareness of the temple will be due to Gentiles having the honor of helping Jesus construct it. Once the passages that cover this are considered, the final chapters of Ezekiel become a simple matter to understand. Zechariah 6:12–13 and 6:15:

> And say to him, "Thus says the LORD of hosts, "Behold, the man whose name is the Branch: for he shall branch out from his place and he shall build the temple of the LORD. It is he who shall build the temple of the LORD and shall bear royal honor, and shall sit and rule on his throne. And there shall be a priest on his throne, and the counsel of peace shall be between them both.""

> And to those who are far off shall come and help build the temple of the LORD. And you shall know that the LORD of hosts has sent me to you. And this shall come to pass, if you will diligently obey the voice of the LORD your God."

After the Jewish people returned from the Babylonian captivity they began to rebuild the temple under the oversight of Zerubbabel the governor and Joshua the high priest. Zechariah used the construction of the second temple as an object lesson on the future coming of the Messiah and the temple that he will build. That the prophet was ultimately looking toward the Messiah is made clear with his reference to *the Branch* (v. 12), a title belonging to the Messiah in relation to him ruling from David's throne (e.g., Jer 23:5; 33:15). It is repeated that the Branch will build the temple of the LORD and rule from his throne. He will enjoy both the offices of king and priest (v. 13), further cementing that the Messiah will fulfill the prophet's words (cf. Gen 14:18; Heb 5:10). Those who live far away from the land of Israel will come to aid in building the temple (v. 15). The Gentiles will bring the wealth of their nations, filling the temple (Hag 2:7). They will be brought to the holy mountain to enjoy equal access to the sanctuary and find joy within. In that day, the temple will be called a house of prayer for all peoples (Isa 56:7).

Shiloh

As Ezekiel was taken to the very high mountain in the land of Israel, he could see that Jerusalem was on the south side of the fifty square mile summit (Ezek 40:2; cf. Ezek 48:8). This suggests that the prophet was coming in from the north, which is where his tour of the temple would soon commence. This places the temple in the Shiloh area, approximately twenty-seven miles north of Jerusalem. Shiloh being on the summit includes it as part of the overall holy district, separated from the world along with Jerusalem. That the Messiah's temple will be in Shiloh, instead of on the traditional temple mount, is not solely based on the need for sufficient space. God said that Shiloh was the place where he made his name to dwell at the first (Jer 7:12). The Tabernacle often rested in Shiloh from about 1375 BC (Josh 18:1) until it was evidently razed by the Philistines after they captured the Ark of the Covenant in 1050 BC (1 Sam 5:1). The Tabernacle was the portable home for the glory of the LORD, making it a proto-temple in its own right. The LORD, through the movement of his glory, would determine where the Tabernacle was erected (Exod 40:35–38; cf. Deut 12:11). This makes Shiloh God's personal choice as his once and future home among his people.

The temple in Shiloh is connected, to a lesser or greater extent, to a key messianic prophecy in Genesis 49:10. Jacob blessed Judah by proclaiming that the right of kingship would never depart from his line, nor would the lawgiver cease until Shiloh comes, and to him will be the obedience of the nations. The meaning of *Shiloh* as used in this verse is uncertain. Some take it as a title for the Messiah, while others understand it as a possessive pronoun, meaning *whose it is*. The problem phrase could also be translated as *until he comes to Shiloh*. If the last option is correct then this well-known passage not only prophesies the Lion from the tribe of Judah as King over all the nations, but even tells us where his house will be.

THE TEMPLE MULTIPLEX

The Outer and Inner Courts

Ezekiel chapters 40–42 concern the measurements of courts, porticos, gates, various rooms, the temple proper, and a description of some instruments and furniture. The details are so specific and numerous that only some of the broader elements and highlights can be examined. As Ezekiel began his tour of the temple, led by a bronze-like guide (Ezek 40:2–4), he was first introduced to the outer court in 40:5–27. The perimeter wall is nearly ten and one-half feet thick and nearly ten and one-half feet high (v. 5). The east gate is described along with adjoining walls, alcoves, a portico, outer and inner thresholds, windows, and steps (vv. 6–16). The portico's doorposts are decorated with palm tree designs (v. 16). The gate complex is gargantuan, measuring a total of about thirty-eight feet wide by seventy-five feet long (vv. 13, 15). Inside the outer court are thirty chambers facing a paved strip (vv. 17–18). The dimension of the outer courtyard, from the front of the lower gate to the front of the exterior of the inner court, measure one hundred and fifty feet (v. 19). The north and south gate complexes are identical to the east gate complex (vv. 20–27).

Next, the prophet provides us with a description of the inner court in Ezekiel 40:28–47. The tour guide showed Ezekiel the three gates to the inner court, this time beginning with the southern gate and ending with the east. Each of the gates substantively match the outer gates, differing only in their porticoes facing out and their stairways consisting of eight rather than seven steps (vv. 31, 34, 37). There are chambers and tables for the purposes of preparing the sacrifices. Because there is a chamber beside the doorpost outside of each inner-court gate (v. 38), then each chamber must be located close to the stairs leading to the portico of the inner gate in the outer court. There are eight tables in total, with four being placed on each side of the gate (v.41). The tables are made of hewn stone, measuring just over two feet long and wide, and one and one-half feet high (v. 42). There are also double hooks of around three inches in length installed all around the house (v. 43). Within the north and east inner gates are two chambers for the priests in the line of Zadok. These chambers are said to be for the priests that also sing (v. 44). They are much like the men that David put in charge of the music ministry in the house of the LORD after the ark was placed there (1 Chr 6:31–32). The chamber facing the south is for the priests that keep charge of the temple (v. 45), while the chamber facing the north is for the priests in charge of the altar (v. 46). The inner court is a square, measuring one hundred and fifty by one hundred and fifty feet. And there, Ezekiel beheld the altar of sacrifice resting in front of the temple (v. 47).

The Temple Proper

A detailed description of the temple building is found in Ezekiel 40:48— 41:26. Ten stairs lead to the temple's entrance, measuring twenty-one feet wide. The entrance utilizes two seven and one-half foot doorposts with a pillar placed beside each one. Once inside, we are greeted by a portico, measuring thirty by eighteen feet (40:48–49). The inner temple is made up of outer and inner sanctuaries. The outer sanctuary is a room measuring thirty by sixty feet with a fifteen foot wide entrance (41:1–2). The entrance to the inner sanctuary measures just nine feet in width (41:3). The outer and inner gates, the entrances to the temple building portico, the entrances to the outer sanctuary, and the inner sanctuary progressively narrow in width. This yields a focusing and purifying effect ending with what the bronze guide refers to as the *Most Holy Place*. This millennial Holy of Holies is a thirty foot square room (41:4). It is the center of worship within the center of worship for all of creation.

A nine foot thick wall surrounds the temple. Next to the wall is a three story structure containing thirty-six foot wide side chambers on each floor. Curiously, the structure is supported by offsets so as not to rely on the wall (41:5–6). The chamber building grows wider as it winds up, resulting in the top floor being the broadest (41:7). This is strong evidence that the millennial temple complex will employ a winding staircase just as Solomon's did (1 Kgs 6:8). The outer wall shared by the side chambers is seven and one-half feet thick. The chambers are all supported by a nine foot high foundation on both sides of the temple (41:8–9). This foundation extends seven and one-half feet beyond the outer wall (41:11). Two doorways facing the north and the south open from the side chambers onto a free space of thirty feet, encircling the temple. This area separates the side chambers from the priest's chambers (41:9–10; cf. Ezek 42:1–14).

A detached building of undisclosed purpose sits next to the western wall of the temple multiplex. It is one hundred and five feet wide by one hundred and thirty-five feet long, with a seven and one-half foot thick wall (41:12). In total, this building measures one hundred and thirty feet long, matching the breadth of the temple's eastern side and the inner courtyard (41:13–15).

The temple is beautifully adorned both inside and out. There are narrow covered windows surrounding the portico, the outer sanctuary, and the inner sanctuary (41:15–16). The inside walls are covered with a wood paneling that reaches the windows (41:16). The entire temple is decorated all around with patterned cherubim and palm tree carvings, similar to those on the walls of Solomon's temple (1 Kgs 6:29). The carvings depict a palm tree between two cherubim, each having two faces. A man's face looks toward the palm on one side while a young lion's face gazes from the other (41:17–20). We are not told what the carvings symbolize. The cherubim might be connected to two of the four living creatures, themselves likely types of cherubim (cf. Ezek 10:15–20), that continuously worship the Lord God Almighty (Rev 4:6–8). The palm trees might typify the triumphal reign of Christ (cf. Matt 21:8–9). Or they may simply be a representation of the physical and spiritual beauty to be enjoyed in the Millennium.

The single piece of furniture within the temple is a four and one-half foot high by three feet in length square wooden altar. The bronze guide identified it as the table that is before the LORD (41:22). This altar is notably smaller than the altar of sacrifice (cf. 43:13–17). Apparently, it is the millennial version of the altar of incense that sat before the veil that separated the Holy Place from the Holy of Holies (Exod 30:6). The smoke rising from the altar of incense pictures the prayers of the saints going up before God (Ps 141:2; Rev 8:3–4).

The outer and inner sanctuary are each fitted with double doors (41:23). Each of the doors are hinged with two leaves (41:24). The cherubim and palm tree carvings are placed on the doors of the outer sanctuary. A canopy of wood is found before the outside portico (41:25). There are narrow windows and palm trees on the sides of the portico (41:26).

The Zadokite Chambers

The two buildings containing chambers for the Zadokite priests are expounded upon in Ezekiel 42:1–14. They are located in the outer court and close to the inner court on the north and south (vv. 1, 3, 10, 13). A detailed description of the northern building is given, along with the notation that the southern building follows the same design (vv. 10–11). The northern building measures one hundred and fifty feet long by seventy-five feet wide (vv. 2, 8). It sits alongside the outer court's pavement (v. 3), with the inner court's northern wall abutting it (cf. Ezek 41:10). A north entrance opens onto a walkway, fifteen feet wide by one hundred and fifty feet long. It runs between the chamber buildings and the corresponding wall on the east (vv. 4, 11–12). Doors to some, if not all, of the rooms are on the northern side (v. 4). The northern building is three stories high, covered in galleries (v. 3). The top floor has more galleries than the middle and base level, resulting in smaller chambers to make up space (v. 5). Unlike the courts, the buildings do not utilize pillars, and so the top story sits back from the lower two (v. 6). In addition to an entrance that faces the north (v. 2), the northern building also has an entrance opening toward the east (v. 9). Before this eastern entrance is a wall parallel to the east side of the building (vv. 7–8). This wall separates the Zadokite priests' chambers from the people in the outer courts. It is a barrier that shelters that which is holy.

These north and south buildings house holy chambers where the priests who approach the LORD prepare for their task. It is in these rooms where they will eat the most holy offerings, the grain and the sin (v. 13). These chambers are also changing rooms, where the priests must leave their holy ministerial garments before exiting into the outer court and among the people (v. 14). The priests are to eat and change clothes in their private buildings to prevent the transmission of holiness to the people (Ezek 44:19; 46:20).

The Overall Dimensions

The bronze guide led the prophet out through the eastern gate to witness the all-around measuring of the temple area in Ezekiel 42:15–20. The east, north, south, and west sides of the outer wall each measure approximately 5,250 feet (vv. 16–19). The outer wall's purpose is to divide the holy within from the common without (v. 20). The temple multiplex is breathtaking in her artistry and symmetry. Properly measured in reeds, her roughly one square mile size (v. 20; cf. Ezek 45:2) is far too large to rest upon the current temple mount. Fortunately, this temple is meant for a time when the wonders of Jesus will be flowing from atop Jerusalem's high and lifted up mountain.

THE SHEKINAH GLORY FILLS THE TEMPLE

In Ezekiel 43:1–5 the prophet is directed to the gate facing the east to witness the returning glory of the LORD! The Shekinah will enter through the eastern gate (v. 4), the same gate from which it had previously departed from Solomon's temple (Ezek 10:18–19; 11:22–23). Its return signals a restoration and reveals much regarding the very purpose of the millennial temple. Ever since Israel's sin drove out the Shekinah from Solomon's temple, it has yet to return. This means that Zerubbabel and Herod's temple never held the same power or status as the first one (cf. Hag 2:3). Israel has been under discipline in some form or another ever since the beginning of the Babylonian Captivity. The Second Coming of Jesus will change all of that, resulting in the ideal relationship between Israel and the LORD (e.g., Acts 3:19–21). The Shekinah will return to a temple far grander than Solomon's, one built under the Messiah's personal rule.

The voice of God as his glory travels from the east is likened to rushing waters (v. 2). The sound and the appearance of this vision remind Ezekiel of his previous one, which depicted the LORD coming to destroy Jerusalem (v. 3). In that vision, Ezekiel had heard rushing water from the cherubim's wings, like the sound of the Almighty, and what appeared to be a glowing fiery metallic man on a sapphire throne. Brilliant light surrounded the figure, radiating around him like a rainbow in the clouds on a rainy day (Ezek 1:24–28). Ezekiel foresaw the same light of the Shekinah glory filling the LORD's house (v. 5). The glory had previously filled the Tabernacle (Exod 40:34–35) and Solomon's temple (1 Kgs 8:10–11; 2 Chr 5:13–14; 7:1–2) after they were erected. This time God's glory will shine across the earth (v.2), and from his home the LORD will give peace (Hag 2:9).

The Glory of the Messiah

The parallels between the departure and return of the Shekinah and those of Jesus are unmistakable. Jesus ascended from and will return to the Mount of Olives (Acts 1:9–12; Zech 14:4), east of Jerusalem. In the Olivet Discourse, Jesus taught that the coming of the Son of Man would be as lightning coming from the east and shining to the west (Matt 24:27). The connection between the Shekinah and the Messiah is profound. At the transfiguration, Jesus' face shone like the sun; his clothes became white as light, and the bright cloud of the Shekinah appeared (Matt 17:2–5). This was a special preview for some of the disciples of what will happen in the millennial kingdom (Matt 16:28; 2 Pet 1:16–18). The earthly reign of the Messiah will manifest God's glory.

The Place of His Throne

The Glory of the LORD had come and departed before. But this time it will never depart from Israel again. Ezekiel 43:7:

> and he said to me, "Son of man, this is the place of my throne and the place of the soles of my feet, where I will dwell in the midst of the people of Israel forever. And the house of Israel shall no more defile my holy name, neither they, nor their kings, by their whoring and by the dead bodies of their kings at their high places,

The Shekinah glory will be in the temple and among the people of Israel forever because he who emanates it will be among them forever. Though it may be a general statement about the abiding glory of the LORD, the language suggests that here is where the Davidic throne will be located. Jesus did say that when he comes in his glory, it is then when he will sit on his glorious throne (Matt 25:31). Additionally, Zechariah 6:13 strongly implies that the Messiah's throne is within the temple. It is fitting that the priestly King would live where the priests performed their functions. There is no doubt that the temple will be the center of the Messiah's rule, which is more important than the physical throne. Wherever the actual throne is, it will be far superior to Solomon's, for Jesus is far superior to Solomon (Matt 12:42). The Messiah's Davidic throne will be more incredible than the one described in 1 Kings 10:18–20:

> The king also made a great ivory throne and overlaid it with the finest gold. The throne had six steps, and the throne had a round top, and on each side of the seat were armrests and two lions standing beside the armrests, while twelve lions stood there, one on each end of a step on the six steps. The like of it was never made in any kingdom.

REVEAL THE DESIGN

Ezekiel 43:6–12 tells of when Israel will be ready for the building of the temple. In Ezekiel's day, the LORD's holy name was defiled through Israel's sins of harlotry, the burial of kings within the temple multiplex area, and the erection of palaces right next to the temple. Israel was implored to put away these detestable practices so that the LORD may dwell among them forever (vv. 7–9). Ezekiel was to describe the temple to the house of Israel so as to make them ashamed of their iniquities and so they could measure the plan (v. 10). Only once the people were ashamed of the sins they had committed could the design and laws of the temple be revealed, so that the design could be observed and the statutes obeyed (v. 11). All of the statutes could be reduced to a simple law: everything on top of Jerusalem's mountain shall be most holy (v. 12).

While the prophet's words were recorded and recognized as inspired by God, they have yet to have any of the prophesied impact on Israel. Only when the people of Israel are ashamed of their sins will they be able to enjoy this temple. That will happen when the Holy Spirit regenerates them as a nation, leading to their recognition of Jesus as the Messiah and thus his return (cf. Zech 12:10; 14:4; Acts 3:19–21). The majestic temple that Ezekiel toured could never exist in the present age. It was always intended for when God's people would be in a pure relationship with him.

WATER FROM THE TEMPLE

The many features that could never be created by man divulges the timing of the temple's construction under the Messiah's kingship. Nevertheless, some imagine that this temple was an offer only for Israel in Ezekiel's day, having no future fulfillment. The deniers have no excuse, for there is an element that is so marvelous that it must be recognized as coming about only by the presence of the Messiah: the river of life flowing from the temple in Ezekiel 47:1–12.

For the sake of this chapter's material, recall that the water will stream from below the house of the LORD's eastern facing threshold (v. 1; Joel 3:18). It begins as only a trickle from the south (v. 2), growing as it flows eastward. The water level is measured in four 1,750 foot deviations, from ankle deep to knee deep to waist deep, becoming so wide and deep that a man could swim in it but could not traverse on foot (vv. 2–5). A literal translation of verse 9 and Zechariah 14:8 teaches that this is a double river, flowing in two directions. One side travels to the Dead Sea and the other to the Mediterranean. Much more detail is given on the side flowing into the Dead Sea. Though it is unlikely the Mediterranean side is much different, if at all.

Several species of fruit trees will grow alongside the banks of the river. These trees will never fail to produce fresh fruit. A new variety will grow every month. Even the leaves are miraculous, never withering, and will be used as medicine (vv. 7, 12). By design, both waterways will run through the farmlands on each side of Jerusalem (cf. Ezek 48:18–19). The river will heal the Dead Sea, making it fresh, and filling it with a great abundance of fish (vv. 8–10). The waters bring life wherever they flow (v. 9). This is a critical aspect to note, for the fountainhead is the very house of the Messiah (v. 12). This river may also serve as a physical reminder of the spiritual living water that Jesus offers (John 4:10–14).

THE ALTAR OF SACRIFICE

The altar of sacrifices' design and statutes for its sanctification are given in Ezekiel 43:13–27. The altar sits in the inner court before the temple proper (Ezek 40:47). The base is one and one-half feet high. It is surrounded by a one and one-half foot wide trench or gutter, with a nine inch high top edge, undoubtedly for draining blood and water (v. 13; cf. 1 Kgs 18:32, 34–35). The base supports three tiers, one on top of another. The first is three feet high and twenty-four feet square (v. 14). The second is six feet high and twenty-one feet square (vv. 14, 17). This tier also has a gutter with a nine inch top edge (vv. 14, 17). The top tier is the hearthstone, measuring six feet high and eighteen feet square. Four horns will extend from the top of its corners (vv. 15–16). Eastward facing steps ascend the altar (v. 17). This creates the first of many contrasts with the Mosaic sacrificial system, within which a staircase climbing the altar was prohibited (Exod 20:26). This altar will be the largest, measuring approximately thirty feet square at its base and eighteen feet in height. Thomas Constable noted that the design makes the altar resemble a small ziggurat.[1]

The cleansing of the altar calls for the first animal sacrifices in the Millennium. This is yet another parallel with the Tabernacle and Solomon's temple in the purification of their sacrificial altars (Exod 29:36–37; Lev 8:15–16; 2 Chr 7:9). On the first of seven days, a young bull is to be brought before the Zadokite priests so that some of the blood can be applied to the altar's four horns, the corners, and the border (vv. 19–20). On the second day, an unblemished male goat is to be sacrificed and used to cleanse the altar in the same manner as the bull (v. 22). On all seven days, a goat, a young bull, and a ram will be prepared as an offering (vv. 21, 23, 25). This process purifies, consecrates, and makes atonement for the altar (v. 26). It will then be ready to receive the burnt and peace offerings, so that God may accept the people (v. 27).

---

1. Constable, *Notes on Ezekiel*, 238.

THE PRIESTHOOD AND SACRIFICIAL SYSTEM

The Shut Gate

Much of Ezekiel chapters 44 through 46 describe the priesthood, the sacrificial system that they will implement, and related matters. In 44:1–3 it is
said that the outer eastern gate is to remain shut because it is through that
entrance that the LORD God of Israel will have entered the temple (vv. 1–2;
cf. Ezek 43:2). The implication is that the LORD and his glory will never
depart from his home or Israel again. The resurrected prince David (cf.
Ezek 34:23–24; 37:24) will have the honor of sitting in the gateway and eat
bread before the Lord Jesus. Because the gate cannot be regularly opened,
the prince will enter through a special porch door (v. 3).

Levitical Caretakers

Ezekiel 44:4–14 concerns the statutes, laws, and holiness that must be observed in the temple. God used the vision of the glory of the LORD filling
the temple to impress upon Ezekiel the importance of these things (v. 4).
Israel was to be reminded of her sin of allowing unbelieving foreigners into
the sanctuary, thereby profaning it, and voiding the covenant (vv. 6–8).
These foreigners were used as caretakers so that the priests could focus on
their more important duties. It is now the Levites, demoted from being
priests, who will become the temple's caretakers (vv. 11, 14). The Levites
must face the consequence of seeking idols instead of God (v. 10). The Levites became a stumbling block of iniquity to Israel, and so they must bear
that shame. They shall not come near to God, for they are no longer priests
(vv. 12–13). How one lives his or her life results in very real repercussions
in the coming kingdom.

Zadokite Priests

Ezekiel 44:15–31 discloses the duties for the only Levites who are allowed
to serve as priests in this regard: the line of Zadok (cf. 1 Chr 6:1–8). In
1 Samuel 2:35 God declared that he would raise up for himself a faithful
priest who would act according to his heart and soul. This priest, later confirmed as Zadok (2 Sam 8:17; 15:24–29), was to be rewarded with an enduring house as he walks before God's anointed forever. God also promised

Zadok's ancestor, Phinehas, that his descendants would become a perpetual priesthood (Num 25:13). The reinstitution of the priestly functions to the Zadokites fulfills God's promises to their forefathers. Before Solomon built the first temple (1 Kgs 6), it was Zadok who anointed him king (1 Kgs 1:39). The house of Zadok has a long and deep history with the LORD's temples. When the rest of Israel went astray, the Zadok family priests remained faithful to their temple duties. They will be rewarded by continuing their faithful temple service, only this time they will be doing so directly before the Messiah in the Messianic Kingdom (v. 15)! They will enjoy access to the LORD's table, ministering to him and keeping his charge (v. 16).

When the Zadokites enter into the inner court they are required to wear linen clothing, including turbans and undergarments. Cotton is forbidden so that the priests can more easily avoid sweating, thereby staying clean as they perform their duties (vv. 17–18). The work clothing must remain in the priest's chambers so that any attached holiness is not taken out among the people (v. 19). The Zadokites are not to shave their heads bald, nor are they allowed to let their hair grow long (v. 20). No doubt this is to symbolize a separation from ancient pagan practices (cf. Lev 21:5, 10). The priests will not be permitted to drink wine when they enter the inner court (v. 21). The inference being that the priests can drink wine when they are off duty. They must marry only Jewish virgins or widows of other priests (v. 22). This rule will keep the Zadokite line pure, signifying separation. What was once only a restriction for the high priest (Lev 21:13–15), will now be required of all the Zadokite priests.

The Zadokites are charged with teaching the people the difference between the holy and profane, resulting in their ability to discern the clean from the unclean (v. 23). The very regulations that the Zadokites will adhere to, allow them to serve as living examples of this kind of separation. They also teach by judging over disputes according to God's rules. The priests will keep God's laws regarding the appointed feasts and they will sanctify his Sabbaths (v. 24). Paul taught that the feasts and Sabbaths were a shadow of what is to come, but their substance is found in Christ (Col 2:16–17). Even with Jesus physically present in the Millennium, the feasts and the Sabbaths will still be important reminders of what is ultimately found only in him.

The priests will only be able to approach a deceased body if it belongs to an immediate family member (v. 25). Even when they do tend to their family member's remains, the priests will still become defiled and must undergo seven days of cleansing (vv. 25–26). When such a priest returns to his duties in the inner court, he must provide a sin offering (v. 27). The people are not to give the Zadokite priests an inheritance or possession of anything in Israel, for God is their inheritance and possession (v. 28). In other words, the priests already have more than they could ever need in what is provided by God. They are to eat the grain offering, the sin offering, and the guilt offering. Every devoted thing in Israel will belong to them (v. 29). They will enjoy the first of the firstfruits, and when the people give the priests the first of their dough, they will receive a blessing on their house (v. 30). The priests are not to eat any bird or animal that died a natural death or was killed by other animals (v. 31). This again underscores the separation unto holiness that the Zadokites represent.

The Prince of Feasts

The prince over Israel is a key millennial figure. His largely feast-centered duties are detailed in Ezekiel 45:9—46:18. In Israel's past she was often ruled by unjust princes that would expropriate property from the people and manipulate the currency (45:9–12). God will no longer allow this with the installment of David as his prince in the Millennium. In some respects, the prince is akin to a high priest. In reality, he is a servant of the great high priest, Jesus, the Son of God (cf. Heb 4:14). The people shall contribute wheat, barley, oil, and sheep to the prince so that he may make atonement for them (45:13–16). This is a ritualistic cleansing atonement and not that which is provided only by the blood of Jesus. It is the prince's role to provide the burnt offerings, the grain offerings, and the drink offerings at all the appointed feasts, including the new moons and the Sabbaths (45:17). It is also David's responsibility to cleanse the temple on the first day of each New Year. Blood from an unblemished young bull must be smeared on the door posts and corners of the house, on the four corners of the altar's ledge, and on the posts of the gate (45:18–19). This is repeated on the seventh day of the first month for all who sin, keeping the house clean and separate from the world (45:20).

The prince will oversee Passover on the 14th of Nisan, the first month. The Passover still lasts seven days and includes the feasts of Unleavened Bread and Firstfruits (45:21; cf. Lev 23:5–10). On the first day of Passover, the prince will provide for himself and all of the people in the land a bull as a sin offering (45:22). On each of the seven days, he will provide seven perfect bulls and seven perfect goats as a burnt offering and a male goat for a sin offering (45:23). A grain offering is required, consisting of one bushel mixed with twelve pints of oil, accompanied by a bull and a ram (45:24).

Passover's observance during the Millennium is quite significant and helpful in understanding these future animal sacrifices. Passover was a shadow of Jesus' sacrifice on the cross and the propitiation effected by his blood, so that God could pass over former sins (Rom 3:23–25). For Jesus was the true Passover lamb (1 Cor 5:7; cf. John 1:29; 1 Pet 1:19). Passover being celebrated even after Jesus returns means that the shadows that once looked forward to his works will become reflections that look back. The millennial Passover requires sacrifices. This indicates that millennial sacrifices overall are for the purpose of pointing back to the shed blood of Jesus as a reminder of his death on the cross for the sins of the world. Regular impactful reminders of what Jesus has done will be on full display. Jesus' victory on the cross will forever be recognized as the focal point of all space and time.

The Feast of Tabernacles is observed on the 15th through the 21st of Tishri, the seventh month. Prince David will provide offerings according to the same pattern as he did for Passover on each of the seven days of Tabernacles (45:25). The majority of the appointed times of Leviticus 23 are identified as being celebrated in the Millennium. None are more emphasized and more explicitly associated with the Millennium than the Feast of Tabernacles. It is mentioned on its own here and almost synonymously with the earthly reign of the Messiah in Zechariah 14:16–19. Saints coming out of the great tribulation to enter the Millennium will be holding palms (Rev 7:9–14), as if to prepare for Tabernacles (cf. Lev 23:40; Neh 8:15). This is in keeping with the idea of the Millennium being the true or archetype Feast of Tabernacles. The Lord Jesus will dwell or tabernacle among his people (e.g., Isa 24:21–23; Zech 14:9; Rev 20:4–6), something that the feast has always been a shadow of.

Israel will observe the Sabbath and the new moon, and it is on those occasions that the east gate of the inner court will be opened (46:1). The gate is to otherwise remain shut with only one exception. The prince may make a burnt or peace offering whenever he likes just as he would on the Sabbath. When he does, the east gate to the inner court will open for him, just as it usually does on the Sabbath (46:12). The prince will enter through his porch door to observe the priests as they provide burnt and peace offerings (46:2). He shall stand in the doorway as he leads the people, gathered just outside, before the LORD in worship (46:3). The prince's offerings for the Sabbath day consist of six unblemished lambs with as much grain as he can give, a single unblemished ram with a bushel of grain, and a bushel with twelve pints of oil (46:4–5, 11). For the new moon, he will offer the same sacrifices with an additional unblemished young bull and a bushel of grain (46:6–7, 11).

When the people approach the LORD during the feasts, they must exit through the gate opposite the one they entered. If a man enters through the north gate then he must leave through the south gate and vice versa (46:9). This results in an easily organized flow of worshippers and allows them to experience more of the temple. The prince will enter and exit when the people do, though he will still make use of his personal entryway (46:8, 10). Every morning the prince will rise to lead the people in worship. He will provide a year old unblemished lamb, about six pints of flour and four pints of oil as a burnt offering (46:13–15).

Prince David may make gifts of inheritance to any of his sons. These gifts will remain theirs because they were given by their father (46:16). The prince may also give gifts to his servants, though they are obliged to return them on the Jubilee year (46:17). The gifts spoken of refer to land, and perhaps items of major importance. This keeps David's priceless property in the family. The prince will not steal from other families, but will only give from what he rightly owns. No longer will the families of Israel be cheated from their land and scattered as they were under the unjust princes of the past (46:18; cf. 45:9).

The reference to David's sons is the only passage we have as to their place in the Millennium. Any of the saved among David's more than twenty sons[2] will be resurrected with their father and serve in his house. This includes the more obvious sons such as Solomon, and on a more touching note, his older brother. Before Solomon, David had a son with Bathsheba who was born sickly. David grieved over his dying son, fasting, and laying all night on the bare ground until the child died on the seventh day (2 Sam 12:15–18). When his son passed, David proclaimed that he would one day go to be with him (2 Sam 12:23). David and his son were reunited in paradise, and they will serve together in the Millennium (cf. Ps 16:10–11).

---

2. David sired nineteen sons through his wives (1 Chr 3:1–9). There was also the first son born from Bathsheba who died in infancy (2 Sam 12:15–18). There was an unspecified number of sons born from various concubines. Jerimoth was another named son (2 Chr 11:18), who may be included in the first list under a different name or was born through a concubine. Tamar was David's only named daughter (1 Chr 3:9).

The Kitchens

The prophet continued his tour as the bronze guide took him to see the kitchens in Ezekiel 46:19–24. He was first led into the chambers that faced north, the building where the priests eat the holiest of the offerings and change their clothes (Ezek 42:13–14). From there, Ezekiel beheld the western end of the building. This is where the priests are to boil the guilt and sin offerings and bake the grain offering (vv. 19–20). These kitchens are kept internal so that the offerings will not have to be taken into the outer court, thus transmitting holiness to the people (v. 20). Ezekiel was then brought into the outer court to view four enclosed little courts, each measuring sixty by forty-five feet, in each corner (vv. 21–22). Lining the inside of each little court is a stone ledge set above cooking hearths (v. 23). It is in these outer-court kitchens where the Levitical caretakers will cook the sacrifices that are for the people to eat (v. 24).

HIS SANCTUARY SHALL RISE

These numerous details on Ezekiel's temple and on the work within require that they be taken seriously. The exact measurements and point by point instruction are nothing like portions of Scripture that are to be understood symbolically, such as the great image in Nebuchadnezzar's dream (Dan 2), or John's vision of the seven horned and seven eyed Lamb (Rev 5). The narrative is far more reminiscent of that provided for the Tabernacle (cf. Exod 25–30), and Solomon's temple (cf. 1 Kgs 6–8), actual physical structures. There is roughly the same amount of instruction provided on the construction of, and the ordinances for, the millennial temple as was given for these other vital sanctuaries. The same kind of phrases used to describe the Shekinah glory dwelling in the millennial temple were used to describe God dwelling in the midst of his people in both the Tabernacle (Exod 25:8), and in Solomon's temple (1 Kgs 6:13). Only this time, the glory of the LORD will dwell among the people of Israel forever (Ezek 43:7). Are we really supposed to conclude that God desired physical dwelling places in the past, but he does not actually mean it when he says the same thing regarding a future home? No respecter of Scripture would deny that the Shekinah departed an actual temple (Ezek 10:18–19; 11:22–23). We should pay the same amount of respect and believe that its return is also to a physical temple (Ezek 43:1–5). All of the intricate design features were not a waste of words, but instructions from God himself. Furthermore, if the future temple and priestly system are just a fantasy then some of God's promises cannot come to pass, such as those he made to Phinehas (Num 25:13) and Zadok (1 Sam 2:35). When Israel is ashamed of her iniquities she will be ready to observe the design of the temple, its laws and its statutes, and carry them out (Ezek 43:10–11).

To conclude, enjoy something that Charles Wesley wrote as part of one of his hymns, which his brother, John Wesley, included in his hymnal:

> We know, it must be done,
> For God hath spoke the word,
> All Israel shall their Saviour own,
> To their first state restor'd:
> Re-built by his command,
> Jerusalem shall rise,
> Her temple on Moriah stand
> Again, and touch the skies.[3]

---

3. Wesley and Wesley, *Collection of Hymns*, 424.

8

Sacrifices in Harmony

MANY CRITICS OF THE literal, grammatical, historical interpretation of prophecy attempt to discredit the hermeneutic by claiming that to believe in future animal sacrifices results in heresy and/or contradiction. Let it be made clear: it is never a heresy to hold to authorial intent or to take God's word at face value. If anything, it is so often the case that the doubting of God's plain word leads to heresies. The supposed contradiction is with Hebrews 10:1–18 (among other relevant verses), which teaches that the one sacrifice of Jesus Christ is sufficient to cover all sins. Truly, it is impossible for the blood of bulls and goats to take away sin (Heb 10:11). Reconciling future animal sacrifices with the atonement brought by Christ is only a *prima facie* or surface level problem. The sacrifices performed in the millennial temple are in full harmony with that of Jesus. Their simultaneous realities in no way discredit the literal interpretation of Scripture, including prophecy. To some, this harmony is not immediately evident. Some explanation is helpful, and at the same time instructive on millennial worship.

THE NATURE OF THE SACRIFICES

What needs to be immediately recognized is that the sacrifice of animals never provided the propitiation that resulted in eternal life. Alva McClain explained, *to the objection that a renewal of 'expiatory' animal sacrifices is unthinkable and would deny the complete efficacy of our Lord's atoning death, the reply is very simple: no animal sacrifice in the Bible has ever had any expiatory efficacy.*[1] The blood of the animals simply had, and will have, a different purpose. There is a universe of difference, in both substance and power, between the blood of the Messiah and the blood of sacrificial animals. This certainly will not change in the Millennium. Even with this in mind, an understanding of the matter based on Hebrews 10 alone could lead to the conclusion that there would be no need for any future animal sacrifices. However, to understand an issue completely we must look to all Scripture has to say on the matter. Ezekiel is just as much a part of God's word as Hebrews is. The prophet's writings are inspired and cannot be read as meaning anything other than what they plainly say unless there is a clear and distinct internal mandate to do so.

Ezekiel 43:18–27 speaks directly to the nature of the sacrifices that will occur. The passage begins with God telling the prophet that on the day the altar is built that burnt offerings are to be made, in addition to sprinkling blood upon it (v. 18). Blood from a young bull is to be put on the altar's horns, on its corners, and on the border around it (vv. 19–20). Placing blood on the altar in this way is to make *atonement* for it (v. 20). The atonement here could either mean that the altar has been saved and has eternal life, or it could just mean that the LORD can accept it. Because the altar is an inanimate object, this type of atonement obviously indicates the latter option. Various uses of atonement do not all speak to that which Jesus provides those who believe on him. And so it is with Ezekiel's use of atonement in his narrative on temple sacrifices.

Any normal reading of the Old Testament lends to the understanding that the blood from animal sacrifices only provided a meager and limited form of atonement when compared to the blood of the Messiah. On this inferior form of atonement, Lewis Sperry Chafer warned that it should not be *invested with New Testament ideas, which contemplate a finished or completed work.*[2] As such, it is certainly not a contradiction to say that atonement will occur by the blood of animals during the Millennium. If it was, then it would follow that all animal sacrifices in the Old Testament contradict the atoning death of Jesus. For his single sacrifice was for all time (Heb 10:12, 14), flowing not only into the future, but also into the past.

Ezekiel further discussed the sacrifice of a goat and how the same use of its blood is supposed to follow the pattern of the bull in cleansing the altar (v. 22). There are still more animals that must undergo ritual acts,

1. McClain, *Greatness of the Kingdom*, 250.
2. Chafer, *Systematic Theology Volume 7*, 25.

including burning and salting (vv. 21, 23–25). After seven days of animal sacrifices the altar is finally consecrated (v. 26). Afterward, the priests are to offer burnt and peace offerings every day. As long as the sacrifices are maintained the LORD God will accept the people (v. 27). This is useful in understanding the millennial sacrifices, because it is clear that they result in the LORD simply accepting certain people in a limited manner and for a limited time. It does not in any way teach that they have now gained the same sort of propitiation as one would through the blood of the Messiah.

CONSISTENCY OF ACCOUNTS

The sacrifices described in Ezekiel are an integral part of the narrative. If they are not to be taken literally then much of the final chapters of the book must be understood allegorically or as vaguely symbolic. Ezekiel would then become a very unusual book, as it is doubtful that the animal sacrifices discussed in relation to previous temples or the Tabernacle would be taken as allegory by any Bible scholars. Furthermore, Ezekiel's description of sacrifices correspond quite well with other prophetic accounts on the matter. At least four other prophets touch on these sacrifices to some extent. The following examples cement the fact that the millennial sacrifices are a uniform teaching. To dismiss all of their words as meaning something other than what they plainly say would result in several detailed swaths of Scripture being neglected or abused.

Conformity with Isaiah

In Isaiah 56:6–8, the prophet wrote of Gentiles partaking in the blessings of the Millennial Kingdom:

> "And the foreigners who join themselves to the LORD, to minister to him, to love the name of the LORD, and to be his servants, everyone who keeps the Sabbath and does not profane it, and holds fast my covenant—these I will bring to my holy mountain, and make them joyful in my house of prayer; their burnt offerings and their sacrifices will be accepted on my altar; for my house shall be called a house of prayer for all peoples." The Lord God, who gathers the outcasts of Israel, declares, "I will gather yet others to him besides those already gathered."

Some Gentiles will work right alongside the Jewish people in serving and loving the name of the LORD (v. 6). This is exactly the kind of equality we would expect among those in the New Covenant. However, it would have been an unthinkable partnership in Isaiah's day. Gentiles will be brought to Jerusalem's mountain, being made joyful in the temple as they offer sacrifices. These offerings are distinctly said to be acceptable on the LORD's altar. In that day, the temple will be known as a house of prayer for every nation (v. 7). This level of participation in temple ordinances is quite astonishing. There is no other time in history in which Gentiles could make legitimate sacrifices in the temple. Sacrifices were previously not even acceptable from an Israelite who was not also a Levite (cf. Deut 33:10). Recall that when Saul attempted a sacrifice, God removed his throne (1 Sam 13:9–14). King Uzziah was struck with leprosy because he offered incense to the LORD (2 Chr 26:18–21). Because Gentile sacrifices have not yet been accepted, it can only be that they will be so in the future. Previously, you were either born a Levite or you were not. During the Millennium, God will make new priests and Levites (Isa 66:21). He will not only ingather the dispersed of Israel but will add to them ingathered Gentiles (v. 8). Ezekiel placed this final ingathering of the Jews and their inclusion in the New Covenant shortly before he covered the future sacrifices (Ezek 36:24–27). Isaiah's narrative on temple sacrifices complements Ezekiel's remarkably well, assuring us that the prophets agree.

A peculiar account that speaks of millennial sacrifices happening elsewhere is found in Isaiah 19:18–21:

> In that day there will be five cities in the land of Egypt that speak the language of Canaan and swear allegiance to the LORD of hosts. One of these will be called the City of Destruction. In that day there will be an altar to the LORD in the midst of the land of Egypt, and a pillar to the LORD at its border. It will be a sign and a witness to the LORD of hosts in the land of Egypt. When they cry to the LORD because of oppressors, he will send them a savior and defender, and deliver them. And the LORD will make himself known to the Egyptians, and the Egyptians will know the LORD in that day and worship with sacrifice and offering, and they will make vows to the LORD and perform them.

The five cities represent the whole of Egypt in the millennial day of the LORD. All of the inhabitants will speak Hebrew, the language of the Promised Land (v. 18). The City of Destruction, likely called so on account of the blood previously spilled there, is referred to as the City of the Sun in the Dead Sea Scrolls, the Targumim, and some other manuscripts. This is Heliopolis, a city where sacrifices used to be made to the sun-god Ra. In the Millennium an altar will be erected, not for Ra, but for the LORD God (v. 19). The altar will serve as a tribute and memorial to the LORD out of gratitude for him sending Egypt a Savior, the Messiah Jesus (v. 20). This follows the pattern of Abraham and Joshua building altars to the LORD out of appreciation and commitment to him (Gen 12:8; Josh 24:26–27), and that of Jacob raising a stone pillar in honor of his covenant with God (Gen 28:18–22). The LORD will reveal himself to the Egyptians and they will come to personally know him. They will worship their Creator with sacrifices and offerings (v. 21). A city that was once dedicated to offering sacrifices to a false god will be repurposed for the offering of sacrifices to the one true God. The Egyptians will not make these offerings to point to what the Savior will do, but out of remembrance for what he has done.

Conformity with Jeremiah

A key passage on the sacrifices relating to the Messiah reigning from David's throne is found in Jeremiah 33:14–18:

> "Behold, the days are coming, declares the LORD, when I will fulfill the promise I made to the house of Israel and the house of Judah. In those days and at that time I will cause a righteous Branch to spring up for David, and he shall execute justice and righteousness in the land. In those days Judah will be saved, and Jerusalem will dwell securely. And this is the name by which it will be called: 'The LORD is our righteousness.' "For thus says the LORD: David shall never lack a man to sit on the throne of the house of Israel, and the Levitical priests shall never lack a man in my presence to offer burnt offerings, to burn grain offerings, and to make sacrifices forever."

A promised time of future blessing is coming, in which the King Messiah, a descendant of David, will rule in justice and righteousness on the earth (vv. 14–15; cf. Jer 23:5). Israel will finally be able to live in safety by virtue of the righteous Messiah ruling in Jerusalem (v. 16; cf. Jer 23:6). Jesus will fulfill the Davidic Covenant by sitting on the throne of the house of Israel (v. 17; cf. 2 Sam 7:13). This results in the priests always having a man to present burnt and grain offerings and sacrifices before (v. 18). Clearly the Messiah will not treat these sacrifices as somehow contradicting what he has done on the cross. Verse 17 is broadly believed to confirm the Davidic Covenant based on what it plainly says. The rest of the statement into verse 18 should be believed based on what it plainly says. The text continues with the LORD telling Jeremiah that if he could disrupt the cycles of day and night, then the Davidic Covenant could also be broken (Jer 33:19–21). The idea of the covenant being broken is presented as an absurdity. And the sacrifices are a direct result of the Davidic Covenant being fulfilled.

Conformity with Zechariah

The book of Zechariah examines several facets of eschatology, including the millennial sacrifices. Zechariah 14:20–21:

> And on that day there shall be inscribed on the bells of the horses, "Holy to the LORD." And the pots in the house of the LORD shall be as the bowls before the altar. And every pot in Jerusalem and Judah shall be holy to the LORD of hosts, so that all who sacrifice may come and take of them and boil the meat of the sacrifice in them. And there shall no longer be a trader in the house of the LORD of hosts on that day.

Everything will be so holy in the millennial Jerusalem that even the common cooking pots will be as sacred as the bowls used to sprinkle blood on the altar (v. 20). Anyone offering sacrifices will be permitted to use any cooking pot to boil them in (v. 21). Zechariah 14 prophesies the Second Coming (v. 4), and the inauguration of the Messiah as King over all the earth (v. 9). During his reign, representatives from the nations must travel to the city annually to celebrate the Feast of Tabernacles. Those nations ignoring this mandate to worship the King during this period will cease to have any rain fall on their land (vv. 16–17). It will be a curse on them just as the plagues were on Egypt (vv. 18–19). This illustrates that unbelievers living in the Millennium can keep God's anger at bay through obedience. Coming to worship the Messiah is a way to keep God from punishing them. By applying this same line of reasoning to the verses that follow, it is reasonable to conclude that the millennial sacrifices may also keep God's wrath away for a short period.

Conformity with Malachi

Finally, Malachi also mentions what can only be millennial sacrifices in 3:1–4:

> *"Behold, I send my messenger, and he will prepare the way before*
> *me. And the Lord whom you seek will suddenly come to his temple;*
> *and the messenger of the covenant in whom you delight, behold, he*
> *is coming, says the LORD of hosts. But who can endure the day of*
> *his coming, and who can stand when he appears? For he is like a*
> *refiner's fire and like fullers' soap. He will sit as a refiner and purifier*
> *of silver, and he will purify the sons of Levi and refine them like*
> *gold and silver, and they will bring offerings in righteousness to the*
> *LORD. Then the offering of Judah and Jerusalem will be pleasing to*
> *the LORD as in the days of old and as in former years.*

Like so many other prophets, Malachi spoke of the First and Second Coming in the same narrative. The messenger that prepared the way before the LORD was John the Baptist (Matt 11:7–10; cf. Isa 40:3; John 1:23). The sudden coming of the Messiah to his temple describes a future event (v. 1; cf. Ezek 43:1–5; Zech 8:3). After the Messiah returns, he will be a purifier of the sons of Levi (vv. 2–3). He will burn off the priesthood's impurities and wash them clean. This will bestow upon them the righteousness that will be required in presenting sacrifices before the LORD (v. 3).[3] The sacrifices will please the LORD as they did before the priesthood became the corrupted class Malachi knew (v. 4). The prophet expected a time in which sacrifices will be reinstituted in a state of purity, taking place after the coming of the Lord Jesus and under his auspices.

A RETURN TO THE MOSAIC COVENANT?

In more than satisfactorily answering this question, Thomas Ice explained:

> *We do not believe that re-instituting sacrifices in a future dispen-*
> *sation will be a return to the Mosaic system of the Old Covenant.*
> *The Mosaic Law has forever been fulfilled and discontinued through*
> *Christ (Rom. 6:14–15; 7:1–6; 1 Cor. 9:20–21; 2 Cor. 3:7–11; Gal.*
> *4:1–7; 5:18; Eph. 2–3; Heb. 7:12; 8:6–7, 13; 10:1–14). The millen-*
> *nium will be a time in which Israel's New Covenant will become*
> *the ruling jurisdiction (Deut. 29:4; 30:6; Isa. 59:20–21; 61:8–9; Jer.*
> *31:31–40; 32:37–40; 50:4–5; Ezek. 11:19–20; 16:60–63; 34:25–26;*

---

3. The sons of Levi descending through Zadok will present the sacrifices (Ezek 45:15) while the rest of the Levites will serve as temple caretakers (Ezek 44:11, 14).

36:24–32; 37:21–28; Zech. 9:11; 12:10–14). Therefore, it will not be a time of returning to the old but of going forward to the new. "For when the priesthood is changed, of necessity there takes place a change of law also" (Heb. 7:12).[4]

Ice identified a glaring fallacy of composition: just because the sacrifices will be reinstituted does not mean that the entirety of the Mosaic Covenant will be as well. The New Covenant made the Mosaic Covenant obsolete (Heb 8:13). The verses provided by Ice make it plain that the New Covenant is the governing agreement over law and practice in the Millennial Kingdom. In fact, sacrifices being made under the New Covenant reveal their distinction and unique purposes in a radically different age. And what is done under the New Covenant cannot be rightly understood as a return to the Mosaic, for the two are incompatible.

The sacrifices described in Ezekiel are quite different than those administered under the Mosaic Covenant. Many of these differences are made apparent when juxtaposing the consecration of the altar in Exodus 29 against the consecration of the altar in Ezekiel 43:18–27. For example, in the Mosaic system, no goats were offered, while in the Ezekiel system a goat is offered on each of the seven days (Ezek 43:25). Another example is that the Mosaic called for applying blood on the horns of the altar (Exod 29:12), while Ezekiel's instruction goes further with the blood also being applied to the corners and on the border around it (Ezek 43:20).

Other differences between the two sacrificial systems are found throughout Scripture. Most notably is that in the Mosaic System the Ark of the Covenant played a critical role, while it will not be missed or even remembered in the Millennium (Jer 3:16). The Ark was only ever a placeholder for the Messiah. In the Mosaic, only the high priest could enter the Holy of Holies (e.g., Heb 9:7). In Ezekiel's system, all priests are permitted to enter (Ezek 44:15–16). In the Mosaic, only a Levite could be a priest, while Isaiah prophecies a time when Gentiles will occupy the office (Isa 66:18–21). In the Mosaic, Passover ordinances were performed by the male head of house (Exod 12:3), while Ezekiel mandates that the Prince oversees the feast for the nation as a whole (Ezek 45:21–24). There are still many more differences to be observed in Ezekiel.[5] *It was these very differences that*

4. Ice, "Why Sacrifices in the Millennium," lines 17–25.

5. Arnold Fruchtenbaum lists some of these examples and more in *The Footsteps of the Messiah*, 456–457.

kept the rabbis from accepting Ezekiel into the Hebrew Canon for some time.[6] These differences highlight the fact that the prophet foresaw a new system and not a return to the old.

TWO PURPOSES

As a Memorial

The first of two likely purposes for sacrifices in the Millennium is that they are performed as a memorial of Jesus' death on the cross. John Whitcomb explained:

> *Even in the age of grace, God deems it necessary for Christians to be reminded of the awful price that Jesus paid, through the symbolism of the bread and the cup. Drinking of this "cup of blessing" (1 Cor. 10:16) does not involve a re-offering of the blood of Christ in contradiction to the Book of Hebrews, but serves as a powerful "remembrance" of Christ and a powerful proclaiming of "the Lord's death till he come" (1 Cor. 11:25–26). Likewise, in the context of distinctive Israelite worship, the five different offerings, four of them with blood-shedding, will serve as a constant reminder to millennial Jews (who will not yet be glorified) of the awful and complete sacrifice which their Messiah, now present in their midst, had suffered centuries before to make their salvation possible. In view of the fact that there may be no other bloodshed in the entire world, because of a return of semi-Edenic conditions (cf. Isa. 11:6–9), such sacrifices upon the Temple altar would be doubly impressive.*[7]

In the observance of the Lord's Supper we demonstrate the death of Jesus as a way to remind us of what he has done. Likewise, the millennial sacrifices will look back to the death of the Messiah, just as the Mosaic sacrifices looked forward. After faith, so much of what God wants from us is to simply remember him and his deeds. Future temple offerings will take the principle behind observing communion and put it on full display before the world. No one will be able to ignore the regular spilling of blood in a world otherwise free of such violence.

The biblical evidence for shadows that looked forward to the works of the Messiah later becoming reflections that look back at them is not limited to Communion observance. Passover was a picture of the blood of Jesus

6. Fruchtenbaum, *Footsteps of the Messiah*, 456.

7. Whitcomb, "The Millennial Temple of Ezekiel 40–48," 21.

becoming a mercy seat for those who received him by faith (e.g., Rom 3:23–25). Passover will be observed in the Millennium and it will require sacrifices (Ezek 45:21–24). Passover pointing to the shed blood of the Messiah will not change and the animal blood will play a part in that remembrance. This signals that the animal sacrifices in general are for the same overall purpose. Paul taught that both the feasts and the Sabbaths are shadows of the things to come; their substance belongs to Christ (Col 2:16–17). The apostle also wrote that it was still acceptable to observe them (Rom 14:5). Some feasts and Sabbaths were not rendered useless simply because Jesus had fulfilled what they were looking forward to. The feasts and Sabbaths will be observed in the Millennium (e.g., Ezek 44:24; Zech 14:16), serving as reflections of the Messiah's great works. It is most reasonable to conclude that the millennial sacrifices will also continue to point to the Messiah.

Horatius Bonar, the 19th century Scottish minister and hymn writer, ended his treatment of this subject with the following powerful summation:

> The temple, the worship, the rites, the sacrifices, have all their centre in the Lamb that was slain. To Him they point, and to Him they speak. Why should they not be allowed to do so in the millennial age, if such be the purpose of the Father? They are commemorative not typical. They are retrospective then, not prospective, as of old. And how needful will retrospection be then, especially to Israel? How needful, when dwelling in the blaze of a triumphant Messiah's glory, to have ever before them some memorial of the cross, some palpable record of the humbled Jesus, some visible exposition of his sin-bearing work, in virtue of which they have been forgiven, and saved, and loved,-to which they owe all their blessedness and honour,-and by means of which, God is teaching them the way in which the exceeding riches of His grace can flow down to them in righteousness. And if God should have yet a wider circle of truth to open up to us out of His word concerning His Son, why should he not construct a new apparatus for the illustration of that truth?[8]

As a Hedge against Defilement

The second likely purpose for sacrifices in the Millennium is that they will appease God's wrath for a time and keep his home pure in the midst of a still sinful world. The most operative passage on this topic is Ezekiel 45:18–20:

8. Bonar, *Coming and Kingdom*, 222–223.

> *"Thus says the LORD God: In the first month, on the first day of the month, you shall take a bull from the herd without blemish, and purify the sanctuary. The priest shall take some of the blood of the sin offering and put it on the doorposts of the temple, the four corners of the ledge of the altar, and the posts of the gate of the inner court. You shall do the same on the seventh day of the month for anyone who has sinned through error or ignorance; so you shall make atonement for the temple.*

On the first day of the year, the blood of a perfect bull must be used to cleanse the temple (vv. 18–19). This suggests that over the previous year, the sin from outside will begin to dirty the temple. The same ritual is repeated six days later to atone for those sins committed out of ignorance or by accident (v. 20). This not only reminds us that the Messiah must keep his home separate, but also that the annual making of atonements or house cleanings are only temporarily effective.

When the Messiah returns he will do so as the Lion (Rev 5:5), ruling with a rod of Iron (e.g., Rev 19:15). He will not allow sin to go unchecked in the same realm where his holiness will reside. Put simply, the King will not tolerate sin in the kingdom. And yet, there will be sinners living throughout the Millennium. This includes children born to parents that do not have glorified bodies (Isa 65:20; Ezek 47:22), thus retaining their sin nature (cf. Rom 5:12). In explaining how the blood of the Messiah purifies the conscience from dead works, animal sacrifices were said to ritually purify the flesh (Heb 9:9–10, 13–14). Just as the offering of animals will continue to point to the Messiah, so too will they continue to provide atonement in the form of ritual cleansing. The sacrifices in this regard are essentially a hedge against defilement that allows for sinful people to live in the Messiah's world until the sin-free Eternal State commences.

GOD HAS SPOKEN

Messianic Temple experts John Schmitt and Carl Laney wrote, *Ezekiel himself believed it was a reality and the future home of Messiah. Then, it becomes not heresy to believe that a Temple and sacrifices will exist; rather, it is almost a heresy to not believe this, especially because it is a part of God's infallible word. The burden on us is to determine how it fits—not its reality.*[9] The profoundly simple reason to accept that there will be sacrifices in the

9. Schmitt and Laney, *Messiah's Coming Temple*, 181.

millennial temple is because God said there would be. It is a colossal special plea to dismiss all of the temple and sacrificial accounts as general allegories or vague "spiritual" teachings, from which any details are of little or no interest. This does not afford Scripture the respect it deserves. It is not the role of the student of Scripture to figure out why what God said is not really what he said (cf. Gen 3:1). Instead, the student should seek to understand how what God says fits together. Only then, will he or she come to appreciate God's word as a whole.

9

Premillennialism in the Early Church

THE ANTE-NICENE AGE REFERS to the period beginning with the death of the apostles and ending with the First Council of Nicaea and the adoption of the original Nicene Creed in AD 325. It is difficult to overstate the significance of the ante-Nicene period in strengthening the unity of believers on key doctrines. It is during this time that the belief in Chiliasm, the early name for Premillennialism, was exceedingly common. In fact, there are no extant writings from a single orthodox Christian during the first two centuries that explicitly support any other interpretation of the Millennium. Many great historians and churchman can be cited in affirming the early dominance of Premillennialism, whether they were themselves of that view or not.

Among them is the celebrated church historian Philip Schaff. He penned this oft quoted passage:

> *The most striking point in the eschatology of the ante-Nicene age is the prominent chiliasm, or millenarianism, that is the belief of a visible reign of Christ in glory on earth with the risen saints for a thousand years, before the general resurrection and judgment. It was indeed not the doctrine of the church embodied in any creed or form of devotion, but a widely current opinion of distinguished teachers, such as Barnabas, Papias, Justin Martyr, Irenaeus, Tertullian, Methodius, and Lactantius . . .* [1]

Schaff did not exaggerate in how prominent Premillennialism was in the ante-Nicene church. If anything, his assessment was quite conservative

---

1. Schaff, *History of the Christian Church Volume II*, 614.

when all of the fathers' writings are considered. While Scripture alone holds supreme authority in the life of the child of God, if a teaching was dominant in the early church then it needs to be seriously considered. For the generations just following the apostles were closer to their teachings and historical context than those in the modern age. What follows is a brief survey of the premillennial beliefs of several key ante-Nicene fathers.

BARNABAS

The *Epistle of Barnabas* was written around 100 AD, and is attributed to one *Barnabas*. Tradition identifies the writer as an Alexandrian Jew living during the time of Trajan and Hadrian. His name may have actually been Barnabas, though it is just as likely that the epistle was named after an apostle to give it some authority. Some, such as Archbishop William Wake, have argued that this Barnabas actually was the apostle.[2]

The Sexta-Septamillennial Construct

Contained in Barnabas' epistle is this common early church millennial belief:

> Attend, my children, to the meaning of this expression, "He finished in six days." This implieth that the Lord will finish all things in six thousand years, for a day is with Him a thousand years. And He Himself testifieth, saying, "Behold, to-day will be as a thousand years." Therefore, my children, in six days, that is, in six thousand years, all things will be finished. "And He rested on the seventh day." This meaneth: when His Son, coming [again], shall destroy the time of the wicked man, and judge the ungodly, and change the-sun, and the moon, and the stars, then shall He truly rest on the seventh day. Ye perceive how He speaks . . . I shall make a beginning of the eighth day, that is, a beginning of another world.[3]

This is a fine example of the doctrine known as the *sexta-septamillennial construct*. The basic idea is that because God created the world in six days and rested on the seventh, there will be six thousand years of earth's existence before the Millennium. This doctrine is derived from Psalm 90:4,

---

2. Roberts et al., *Ante-Nicene Fathers Volume I*, 133.

3. Ibid., 146–147. Barnabas, *The Epistle of Barnabas*, Chapter XV.

Jubilees 4:29–30, and especially 2 Peter 3:8. The days of creation from Genesis 1 are understood in light of Peter's explanation of days being to God as millenniums, with the reversal also being true. The seventh millennium is looked to as the ultimate fulfillment of the Sabbath, for it is the seventh *day*. Only after the seven *days* have been completed, will the eighth *day* or the Eternal State commence. Premillennialism is not at all dependent on the sexta-septamillennial construct. It is the construct that relies on Premillennialism for support. According to the solar calendar the construct has been proven false. It is still possible according to the Hebrew calendar, which has not yet reached the year 5800. Regardless of the doctrine's veracity, its prevalence highlights the importance many in the early church put on the literal thousand years of Revelation 20. Several early fathers were so confident in Premillennialism that they used it as a basis for other ideas, true or not as they may be.

Barnabas believed that the Millennium would only begin after Jesus comes again to destroy the wicked man, i.e., the man of lawlessness (2 Thess 2:3), judge nonbelievers, and modify creation. Barnabas identified these events as taking place toward the end of the six thousandth year of creation.

POLYCARP

Polycarp lived from about AD 65 to 155, and finds himself among the greatest Christians the world has ever witnessed. He was a friend of and fellow pupil alongside Ignatius, under the apostle John. Archbishop James Ussher identified Polycarp as the angel of the church in Smyrna,[4] spoken of by Jesus himself in Revelation 2:8.[5] This is quite likely given that Polycarp was the pastor of this congregation during the period in which Revelation was written in AD 95–96. The Romans attempted to burn Polycarp at the stake, where before a stadium crowd, the flames miraculously refused to touch him. Finally, Polycarp was martyred when an executioner pierced him with a dagger, resulting in blood spilling out so profusely that it quenched the flames.[6]

---

4. An angel is not always a supernatural being, but can be any kind of messenger or envoy.

5. Ibid., 31.

6. Ibid., 42. *The Encyclical Epistle of the Church at Smyrna*, Chapter XVI.

It is one of the great disappointments of church history that Polycarp's sole extant work is his epistle to the Philippians. In this invaluable letter we find a brief summary of the end times that indicates a premillennial view:

> If we please Him in this present world, we shall receive also the future world, according as He has promised to us that He will raise us again from the dead, and that if we live worthily of Him, "we shall also reign together with Him," provided only we believe. In like manner, let the young men also be blameless in all things . . . since "every lust warreth against the spirit;' and 'neither fornicators, nor effeminate, nor abusers of themselves with mankind, shall inherit the kingdom of God,"[7]

While Polycarp does not specifically mention a period of a thousand years, he does affirm some key distinctives of Premillennialism. Saints are to reign with Jesus only after they are resurrected. In instructing on how to inherit this future age, Polycarp quoted 1 Corinthians 6:9, thereby equating the period after the resurrection with the kingdom. Such teachings would not have been found in any eschatological view outside of Premillennialism.

In defending the blessings to be found in the millennial kingdom, Irenaeus revealed that *the elders who saw John, the disciple of the Lord, related that they had heard from him how the Lord used to teach in regard to these times . . .* [8] Polycarp was a student of the apostle John and the teacher of Irenaeus. This makes it likely that Polycarp was one of these elders that delivered teachings on the Millennium. Irenaeus soon after wrote that the millennial blessings were *borne witness to in writing by Papias, the hearer of John, and companion of Polycarp . . .* [9] This supports the conclusion that Polycarp was one of the premillennial elders, and reminds us that Polycarp was associated with yet another premillennialist in Papias. Even though we have no conclusive evidence that Polycarp held to the complete premillennial system, the circumstantial evidence is compelling.

PAPIAS

Alongside Polycarp, Papias was a student of the apostle John. He was the bishop of Hierpolis in Phrygia, and was martyred around the same time

---

7. Ibid., 34. Polycarp, *the Epistle of Polycarp to the Philippians*, Chapter V.
8. Ibid., 562. Irenaeus, *Against Heresies*, Book V, Chapter XXXIII.
9. Ibid., 563. Irenaeus, *Against Heresies*, Book V, Chapter XXXIII.

as Polycarp in 163 AD. In addition to enjoying friendship with the apostle John, Papias intimately knew several others who had been alive to interact with Jesus and the apostles.[10] This makes Papias among the most important Christian figures following the completion of the Bible. It is unfortunate that outside of a few relics, what survives of Papias' teachings can only be found where he is quoted or paraphrased by other fathers.

Eusebius of Caesarea, an early fourth century church historian, confirmed Papias' Premillennialism:

> *The same person, moreover, has set down other things as coming to him from unwritten tradition, amongst these some strange parables and instructions of the Saviour, and some other things of a more fabulous nature. Amongst these he says that there will be a millennium after the resurrection from the dead, when the personal reign of Christ will be established on this earth.*[11]

Papias expected that Jesus' earthly reign during the Millennium was to commence after the resurrection of the dead. It is of special interest that Eusebius recorded that Papias received this belief from an unwritten tradition. Papias' connection with those who knew Jesus personally indicates that he likely heard of this teaching from one or more of these individuals. It is quite possible that the apostle John himself instructed Papias on the Millennium. This makes the most sense given that John was the writer of Revelation, the book that most clearly teaches on the thousand year reign of Christ.

After writing on the blessings to be found in the Millennium, Irenaeus provided this fascinating quote from Papias:

> *And these things are borne witness to in writing by Papias, the hearer of John, and a companion of Polycarp, in his fourth book; for there were five books compiled (συντεταγμένα) by him. And he says in addition, "Now these things are credible to believers." And he says that, "when the traitor Judas did not give credit to them, and put the question, 'How then can things about to bring forth so abundantly be wrought by the Lord?' the Lord declared, 'They who shall come to these [times] shall see.'"*[12]

---

10. Ibid., 151.

11. Ibid., 154. Eusebius, *Fragments of Papias*, VI.

12. Ibid., 563. Irenaeus, *Against Heresies*, Book V, Chapter XXXIII.

According to Papias, Judas not only doubted the millennial blessings, but even questioned Jesus on how such marvels could ever come to pass. In evoking the villain Judas, Papias and Irenaeus underscored just how important they thought it was to disagree with him.

JUSTIN MARTYR

Perhaps the most overtly premillennial ante-Nicene church father was Justin Martyr. He was a Gentile born around 114, and was martyred in 165 AD. He was a follower of Plato until he became a disciple of Jesus. Justin identified the Gospel as the only true philosophy and he became an evangelist.[13] It would be only be natural for a former Platonist to view the Millennium as something other than literal. Nevertheless, Justin believed the plain words of prophecy on the major points.

The Orthodoxy of Premillennialism

In writing against those who deny the resurrection, Justin gave his most famous statement on the Millennium:

> For if you have fallen in with some who are called Christians, but who do not admit this [truth] and venture to blaspheme the God of Abraham, and the God of Isaac, and the God of Jacob; who say there is no resurrection of the dead, and that their souls, when they die, are taken to heaven; do not imagine that they are Christians . . . But I and others, who are right-minded Christians on all points, are assured that there will be a resurrection of the dead, and a thousand years in Jerusalem, which will then be built, adorned, and enlarged, [as] the prophets Ezekiel and Isaiah and others declare.[14]

Justin was writing to inform Trypho[15] that those who deny the coming resurrection of the saints may call themselves Christians, but their teachings blaspheme God. Justin then affirmed that Christians holding to proper doctrine, not only believe in the resurrection, but also that the Millennium would follow, centered in a glorified Jerusalem. To Justin, the resurrection and the Millennium were natural partners and part of the same overall

---

13. Ibid., 160.

14. Ibid., 239. Justin Martyr, *Dialogue With Trypho*, Chapter LXXX.

15. Likely a fictional Jewish character created by Justin as a literary device.

doctrine. Justin was, though, careful to note that there were genuine Christians who disagreed with him on the Millennium and that Jerusalem would be rebuilt.[16] Though Isaiah and Ezekiel say much on the Millennium, it is likely that Justin had prophecies regarding the great and holy mountain in mind when writing on the enlarged Jerusalem (e.g., Isa 2:2–4; 27:13; 56:6–8; 66:20; Ezek 20:40–41; 40:1–4; 45:1–8; 48:8–20).

In relating the Millennium to the resurrection of the unjust, Justin continued:

> And further, there was a certain man with us, whose name was John, one of the apostles of Christ, who prophesied, by a revelation that was made to him, that those who believed in our Christ would dwell a thousand years in Jerusalem; and that thereafter the general, and, in short, the eternal resurrection and judgment of all men would likewise take place.[17]

Justin reiterated that believers in Christ will live in Jerusalem for a thousand years and that afterward the rest of humanity will be resurrected to face judgment. These two general resurrections bookend the Millennium just as the apostle John recorded in Revelation 20:4–6.

Isaiah 65

After writing, *For Isaiah spake thus concerning this space of a thousand years*, Justin quoted Isaiah 65:17–25.[18] He had no compunction in providing a passage about the Millennium, even if it did not explicitly mention a thousand year period. The church father understood that if Scripture describes a period that does not fit in the present world or in the Eternal State, that it must find its home in the Millennium. This type of inductive reasoning is common among premillennial scholars throughout church history.

Justin further developed the sexta-septamillennial construct by unpacking Jubilees 4:29–30, where it is revealed that Adam died in that *day* because he died before reaching a thousand years of age. Justin treated the tree in Isaiah 65:22 as the Tree of Life, supporting his assertion that the passage obscurely predicts a thousand years. God's people will be enabled to live throughout the entire Millennium. Justin believed that the day of the

---

16. Ibid., 239. Justin Martyr, *Dialogue With Trypho*, Chapter LXXX.
17. Ibid., 240. Justin Martyr, *Dialogue With Trypho*, Chapter LXXXI.
18. Ibid., 240. Justin Martyr, *Dialogue With Trypho*, Chapter LXXXI.

Lord being as a thousand years was connected to this subject (2 Pet 3:8). He concluded that Isaiah 65:17–25 concerned the reversal of the corruption introduced in Genesis 2:17 and chapter 3.[19]

IRENAEUS

Irenaeus lived from AD 120 to 202, serving as the bishop of the church in what is now Lyon France. He was a pupil of Polycarp,[20] himself a student of the apostle John. Irenaeus being only one teacher removed from the disciple whom Jesus loved (e.g., John 13:23), makes the father's extensive writings all the more valuable. His magnum opus, *Against Heresies*, was written to address and defeat the false doctrines and lies of the Gnostics. The last five chapters of book five are so favorable to Premillennialism that they were left out of the Latin translations in the Medieval Era by the doctrine's opponents, only to be supplied again in 1575.[21]

Not surprisingly, Irenaeus held to the sexta-septamillennial construct:

> For in as many days as this world was made, in so many thousand years shall it be concluded. And for this reason the Scripture says: "Thus the heaven and the earth were finished, and all their adornment. And God brought to a conclusion upon the sixth day the works that He had made; and God rested upon the seventh day from all His works." This is an account of the things formerly created, as also it is a prophecy of what is to come. For the day of the Lord is as a thousand years; and in six days created things were completed: it is evident, therefore, that they will come to an end at the sixth thousand year.[22]

He taught that after six thousand year periods, the seventh will follow: the day of the Lord. Some have argued that Irenaeus might have believed that the seventh day was eternal, meaning he was not premillennial. This is easily disproven. Elsewhere, Irenaeus wrote that it is only after the seventh-day kingdom when the New Jerusalem will descend upon the earth.[23] Those who took the mark of the beast are to come to an end at the completion of the sixth thousandth year. To Irenaeus, the mark's number is six hundred

---

19. Ibid., 239–240. Justin Martyr, *Dialogue With Trypho*, Chapter LXXXI.

20. Ibid., 309.

21. Ibid., 313.

22. Ibid., 557. Irenaeus, *Against Heresies*, Book V, Chapter XXVIII.

23. Ibid., 566. Irenaeus, *Against Heresies*, Book V, Chapter XXXV.

and sixty-six because it was a *summing up of the whole of that apostasy which has taken place during six thousand years.*[24]

The Seventh-Day Kingdom

Irenaeus spoke of the seventh-day millennium and the kingdom as being one in the same:

> For what are the hundred-fold [rewards] in this word, the entertainments given to the poor, and the suppers for which a return is made? These are [to take place] in the times of the kingdom, that is, upon the seventh day, which has been sanctified, in which God rested from all the works which He created, which is the true Sabbath of the righteous, which they shall not be engaged in any earthly occupation; but shall have a table at hand prepared for them by God, supplying them with all sorts of dishes.[25]

After quoting from the parable of the great banquet (Luke 14:12–13), Irenaeus asked and answered when these rewards will be given. It will happen during the millennial kingdom, which is also the true Sabbath. Because God rested on the seventh day of creation, the saints will do no work during the Millennium, but will instead enjoy a great banquet prepared for them by God.

The father explained that blessings of this kind could not be found in a heavenly realm but only on the earth after the resurrection:

> [Christ], after he had given thanks while holding the cup, and had drunk of it, and given it to the disciples, said to them: "... But I say unto you, I will not drink henceforth of the fruit of this vine, until that day when I will drink it new with you in my Father's kingdom." Thus, then, He will Himself renew the inheritance of the earth, and will re-organize the mystery of the glory of [His] sons; as David says, "He who hath renewed the face of the earth." He promised to drink of the fruit of the vine with His disciples, thus indicating both on these points: the inheritance of the earth in which the new fruit of the vine is drunk, and the resurrection of His disciples in the flesh. For the new flesh which rises again is the same which also received the new cup. And He cannot by any means be understood as drinking of the fruit of the vine when settled down with his [disciples] above in a super-celestial place; nor again, are they who drink it devoid of

24. Ibid., 557. Irenaeus, *Against Heresies*, Book V, Chapter XXVIII.
25. Ibid., 562. Irenaeus, *Against Heresies*, Book V, Chapter XXXIII.

flesh, for to drink of that which flows from the vine pertains to flesh, and not spirit.[26]

Irenaeus understood that it will be during the kingdom in which Jesus will again drink wine with his disciples. This proves that those in Christ are to inherit the earth, doing so in resurrected bodies. Irenaeus made a cogent point, for Jesus ate fish to prove that he was not merely a spirit but had resurrected in the flesh (Luke 24:41–43). The kingdom is realized after the resurrection, when Jesus will renew the face of the earth (Ps 104:30).

Against Allegory

One of the key reasons for Irenaeus' Premillennialism is that he was convinced that prophecy must be understood plainly. In criticizing those who interpret otherwise, he wrote:

> *If, however, any shall endeavour to allegorize [prophecies] of this kind, they shall not be found consistent with themselves in all points, and shall be confuted by the teaching of the very expressions [in question]. For example: "When the cities" of the Gentiles "shall be desolate, so that they be not inhabited, and the houses so that there shall be no men in them and the land shall be left desolate." For, behold," says Isaiah, "the day of the LORD cometh past remedy, full of fury and wrath, to lay waste the city of the earth, and to root sinners out of it." And again he says, "Let him be taken away, that he behold not the glory of God." And when these things are done, he says, "God will remove men far away, and those that are left shall multiply in the earth." "And they shall build houses, and shall inhabit them themselves: and plant vineyards, and eat of them themselves." For all these and other words were unquestionably spoken in reference to the resurrection of the just, which takes place after the coming of Antichrist, and the destruction of all nations under his rule; in [the times of] which [resurrection] the righteous shall reign in the earth.*[27]

Irenaeus quoted from Isaiah 6:11; 13:9; 26:10; 6:12; and 65:21. He required just one book to make his point that there are numerous prophecies that can only be fulfilled when the righteous will rule the earth. This rule can only happen after the rise and fall of the Antichrist and the resurrection of the saints. Those who disagree with Irenaeus' placement of when such

---

26. Ibid., 562. Irenaeus, *Against Heresies*, Book V, Chapter XXXIII.

27. Ibid., 565. Irenaeus, *Against Heresies*, Book V, Chapter XXXV.

prophecies will come to pass must resort to allegory to make them fit elsewhere. The father warned that those who do this do not even find consistency among themselves and are refuted by the very verses they abuse.

His reason for taking prophecy plainly is summed up with:

> *and nothing is capable of being allegorized, but all things are stedfast, and true, and substantial, having been made by God for righteous men's enjoyment. For as it is God truly who raises up man, so also does man truly rise from the dead, and not allegorically . . . For since there are real men, so must there also be a real establishment*[28]

The Abrahamic Covenant

Irenaeus perceived the times of the Millennium as being based in Jerusalem. This was predicated on the land promise in the Abrahamic Covenant:

> *Thus, then, the promise of God, which He gave to Abraham, remains stedfast . . . Thus he did await patiently the promise of God, and was unwilling to appear to receive from men, what God had promised to give him, when He said again to him as follows: "I will give this land to thy seed, from the river of Egypt even unto the great river Euphrates." If, then, God promised him the inheritance of the land, yet he did not receive it during all the time of his sojourn there, it must be, that together with his seed, that is, those who fear God and believe in Him, he shall receive it at the resurrection of the just.*[29]

He reasoned that if God made a promise, and it has not yet come to pass, then it must yet be future. Only after Abraham is resurrected will he and his seed finally inherit all of the Promised Land. Irenaeus elaborated in writing that Israel will be gathered from all the nations and dwell in the land that was promised to Jacob.[30] The apocryphal book of Baruch 4:36—5:9 was quoted in its entirety to support that the rule of the saints will be centered in Jerusalem.[31] This section of Baruch anticipates Jerusalem standing on high, when the throne of the kingdom is established and the world is reshaped to suit Israel.

---

28. Ibid., 566. Irenaeus, *Against Heresies*, Book V, Chapter XXXV–XXXVI.
29. Ibid., 561. Irenaeus, *Against Heresies*, Book V, Chapter XXXII.
30. Ibid., 563. Irenaeus, *Against Heresies*, Book V, Chapter XXXIV.
31. Ibid., 565. Irenaeus, *Against Heresies*, Book V, Chapter XXXV.

The father could only recognize such blessings as having a tangible fulfillment:

> Now all these things being such as they are, cannot be understood in reference to super-celestial matters; "for God," it is said, "will show to the whole earth that is under heaven thy glory." But in the times of the kingdom, the earth has been called again by Christ [to its pristine condition], and Jerusalem rebuilt after the pattern of the Jerusalem above, of which the prophet Isaiah says, "Behold, I have depicted thy walls upon my hands, and thou art always in my sight." And the apostle too, writing to the Galatians, says in like manner, "But the Jerusalem which is above is free, which is the mother of us all." [32]

This is just one more example of Irenaeus deriding the relegation of kingdom prophecies to some vague heavenly location or application. He understood the millennial Jerusalem as being based on the original in Heaven, providing Isaiah 49:16 and Galatians 4:26 for support. Concerning the Jerusalem in Heaven Irenaeus wrote, *And in the Apocalypse John saw this new [Jerusalem] descending upon the new earth. For after the times of the kingdom, he says, "I saw a great white throne, and Him who sat upon it . . .* Revelation 21:2 was referenced as being placed just after where John wrote on the kingdom in Revelation. This is another example of the kingdom being equated with the thousand years of Revelation 20. An important distinction is made, not only between the millennial Jerusalem and the heavenly Jerusalem, but also between the Millennium and the Eternal State.

Ecology

Irenaeus began his most significant teaching on the Millennium's ecology by looking to Isaac's blessing of Jacob. After quoting Genesis 27:27–29, the father wrote:

> If any one, then, does not accept these things as referring to the appointed kingdom, he must fall into much contradiction and contrariety . . . For not only did not the nations in this life serve this Jacob; but even after he had received the blessing, he himself going forth [from his home], served his uncle Laban the Syrian for twenty years; and not only was he not made lord of his brother, but he did himself bow down before his brother Esau . . . Moreover, in what way did he inherit much corn and wine here, he who emigrated to Egypt because

---

32. Ibid., 565–566. Irenaeus, *Against Heresies*, Book V, Chapter XXXV.

of the famine which possessed the land in which he was dwelling . . . ?
The predicted blessing, therefore, belongs unquestionably to the times
of the kingdom, when the righteous shall bear rule upon their rising
from the dead; when also the creation, having been renovated and
set free, shall fructify with an abundance of all kinds of food [33]

If nations are to ever bow down to Jacob (Gen 27:29) then he must be resurrected in order for them to do so. It is at this time that God will give him
the dew of heaven, the fatness of the earth and much grain and wine (Gen
27:28).

This led to Irenaeus relaying a non-canonical teaching of Jesus:

the elders who saw John, the disciple of the Lord, related that they
had heard from him how the Lord used to teach in regard to these
times, and say: The days will come in which vines shall grow, each
having ten thousand branches, and in each branch ten thousand
twigs, and in each true twig ten thousand shoots, and in each one
of the shoots ten thousand clusters, and on every one of the clusters
ten thousand grapes, and every grape when pressed will give five and
twenty metretes[34] *of wine. And when any one of the saints shall lay*
hold of a cluster, another shall cry out, "I am a better cluster, take
me; bless the Lord through me." In like manner [the Lord declared]
that a grain of wheat would produce ten thousand ears, and that
every ear should have ten thousand grains, and every grain would
yield ten pounds (quinque bilibres) of clear, pure, fine flour; and that
all other fruit-bearing trees, and seeds and grass, would produce in
similar proportions[35]

Irenaeus believed that in the Millennium there will be multitudes of gargantuan talking grapes! It is this teaching in particular that opponents of
the father's Premillennialism mock him for. However, even if Irenaeus intended for these words to be taken as strictly as possible, which is unlikely,
it is only because he had great faith that the blessing on Jacob will material-
ize in the most wondrous ways imaginable. Not only will grain and wine
become numerous and massive, but the fatness of the earth will likewise
manifest in all produce and kernels. Formerly carnivorous animals will be

33. Ibid., 562. Irenaeus, *Against Heresies*, Book V, Chapter XXXIII.

34. A metrete was a unit of liquid measurement in ancient Greece, equivalent to 37.4
liters.

35. Ibid., 562–563. Irenaeus, *Against Heresies*, Book V, Chapter XXXIII.

sustained by eating from these productions alone, allowing them to be in harmony with and subjection to man.[36]

Isaiah 11:6–8 is provided and then Irenaeus followed with:

> And it is right that when the creation is restored, all the animals should obey and be in subjection to man, and revert to the food originally given by God (for they had been originally subjected in obedience to Adam), that is, the productions of the earth. But some other occasion, and not the present, is [to be sought] for showing that the lion shall [then] feed on straw. And this indicates the large size and rich quality of the foods. For if that animal, the lion, feeds upon straw [at that period], of what a quality must the wheat itself be whose straw shall serve as suitable food for lions?[37]

Irenaeus could not perceive how Isaiah's prophecy could come to pass in the present age. He could only see the plain meaning as applying to the future times of the kingdom and the restoration of creation.

TERTULLIAN

Quintus Septimius Florens Tertullianus, referred to by Jerome as Tertullian, was the father of Latin Christianity and of western theology. He was born sometime between AD 145 to 160 in Carthage, and died sometime between AD 220 to 240. Tertullian was a skilled theologian, with an aptitude for apologetics and polemics against various heresies. His writings are extensive, many of which may not even be extant. Cyprian, an influential church father in his own right, said that he never let a day pass without reading something of Tertullian's.[38] During the last phase of his life Tertullian joined the Montanists, a faction not unlike that of modern-day charismatics and Pentecostals. It was Tertullian who wrote the oldest known formal exposition of the Trinity in *Against Praxeas*, for which the faithful owe him enormous gratitude.

---

36. Ibid., 563. Irenaeus, *Against Heresies*, Book V, Chapter XXXIII.
37. Ibid., 563. Irenaeus, *Against Heresies*, Book V, Chapter XXXIII.
38. Roberts et al., *Ante-Nicene Fathers Volume III*, 5.

The New Jerusalem Variant

In writing against the Marcionite heresy,[39] Tertullian's Premillennialism was disclosed:

> But we do confess that a kingdom is promised to us upon the earth, although before heaven, only in another state of existence; inasmuch as it will be after the resurrection for a thousand years in the divinely-built city of Jerusalem, "let down from heaven," which the apostle also calls "our mother from above;" and, while declaring that our πολίτευμα, or citizenship, is in heaven, he predicates of it that it is really a city in heaven. This both Ezekiel had knowledge of and the Apostle John beheld.[40]

A future kingdom lasting one thousand years was expected to be established upon the earth, taking place after the resurrection of the saints. Tertullian confirmed several other standard tenants, such as the rise and defeat of the Antichrist before the inauguration of the Millennium.[41] He diverged in teaching that at the end of the Millennium the saints will be transferred to Heaven instead of occupying the new earth. Also, Tertullian wrote that it is during the Millennium, and not after, when the New Jerusalem will descend and be occupied. The father interpreted Revelation 21–22:5 as not taking place after chapter 20, but as a supplement providing details on the Millennium. Tertullian's profession was not based on Revelation alone, but also upon Ezekiel.

Tertullian provided a broad timeline and further details:

> Of the heavenly kingdom this is the process. After its thousand years are over, within which period is completed the resurrection of the saints, who rise sooner or later according to their deserts, there will ensue the destruction of the world and the conflagration of all things at the judgment: we shall then be changed in a moment into the substance of angels, even by the investiture of an incorruptible nature, and so be removed to that kingdom in heaven[42]

---

39. In 144 AD Marcion of Sinope crafted a type of dualism that portrayed the God of Israel and the Old Testament as petty and separate from the more powerful and loving God of the New Testament.

40. Ibid., 342. Tertullian, *Against Marcion*, Book III, Chapter XXV.

41. Ibid., 563. Tertullian, *On the Resurrection of the Flesh*, Chapter XXIV.

42. Ibid., 343. Tertullian, *Against Marcion*, Book III, Chapter XXV.

The New Jerusalem is considered to be the heavenly kingdom because it comes from Heaven. There will be more than one resurrection of the saints. In what resurrection a given saint is to partake in is based on the rewards he or she is due. Because Tertullian interpreted the final two chapters of Revelation as occurring during the Millennium, he was able to hold to the subsequent destruction of the world without any refinement or replacement. The conflagration will accompany the judgment, and only then will the saints will be made like angels. Therefore, Tertullian understood Matthew 22:30 and Luke 20:36 as being fulfilled after the completion of the Millennium. This view allows for even resurrected saints to procreate during the Millennium. Tertullian's variant beliefs testify to what a big tent doctrine Premillennialism is.

Heavenly and Earthly Blessings

In covering the Millennium and what follows, Tertullian explained that heavenly and earthly blessings are natural partners:

> What appears to be probable to you, when Abraham's seed, after the primal promise of being like the sand of the sea for the multitude, is destined likewise to an equality with the stars of heaven—are not these the indications both of an earthly and a heavenly dispensation? When Isaac, in blessing his son Jacob, says, "God give thee of the dew of heaven, and the fatness of the earth," are there not in his words examples of both kinds of blessings? . . . So are we first invited to heavenly blessings when we are separated from the world, and afterwards we thus find ourselves in the way of obtaining also earthly blessings.[43]

Tertullian's belief in Premillennialism did not result in him focusing on mere physical blessings, while ignoring the spiritual. On the contrary, Tertullian was able to properly appreciate the spiritual blessings precisely because he did not separate them from the physical.

METHODIUS

Methodius or Eubulius lived from 260–312 AD, serving as bishop of both Olympus and Patara in Lycia. Jerome records that he was transferred to the

---

43. Ibid., 343. Tertullian, *Against Marcion*, Book III, Chapter XXV.

See of Tyre in Phoenicia. He suffered martyrdom at Chalcis in Greece or possibly in Syria. Methodius is best known as a critic of Origen and his allegorical method of interpreting Scripture.[44] Epiphanius made considerable use of Methodius in his own refutation of Origen.[45]

The Feast of Tabernacles

Methodius developed the sexta-septamillennial construct further by dovetailing it in with the Feast of Tabernacles:

> *For since in in six days God made the heaven and the earth, and finished the whole world, and rested on the seventh day from all His works which He had made, and blessed the seventh day and sanctified it, so by a figure in the seventh month, when the fruits of the earth have been gathered in, we are commanded to keep the feast to the Lord, which signifies that, when this world shall be terminated at the seventh thousand years . . . in the seventh month, the great resurrection-day, it is commanded that the Feast of our Tabernacles shall be celebrated to the Lord, of which the things said in Leviticus are symbols and figures*[46]

The Feast of Tabernacles or Sukkot is observed on the 15th through the 21st of Tishri, the seventh month of the ecclesiastical year in the Hebrew Calendar. To Methodius, the sexta-septamillennial construct did not just have implications for days and millenniums, but also for at least one month. The final of the seven feasts of Israel on the seventh month, indicated that it was a shadow of what is yet to be found in the seventh day or the Millennium. Leviticus 23 records all of the feasts of the LORD that Moses was to proclaim to the people of Israel. Methodius understood that these feasts were figures that pointed to greater realities.

Though Methodius does not list how each feast is fulfilled, he specifically identified Passover as the spilling of Jesus' blood on the cross[47] and Tabernacles as the Millennium:

> *For I also, taking my journey, and going forth from the Egypt of this life, came first to the resurrection, which is the true Feast of the Tabernacles, and there having set up my tabernacle, adorned with the*

44. Roberts et al., *Ante-Nicene Fathers Volume VI*, 307.
45. Ibid.
46. Ibid., 344. Methodius, *the Banquet of the Ten Virgins*, Discourse IX, Chapter I.
47. Ibid., 345. Methodius, *the Banquet of the Ten Virgins*, Discourse IX, Chapter I.

*fruits of virtue, on the first day of the resurrection, which is the day
of judgment, celebrate with Christ the millennium of rest, which is
called the seventh day, even the true Sabbath.*[48]

The Millennium is not just the seventh day and the true Sabbath, but also
the true Feast of Tabernacles, beginning with the resurrection on the first
day. The tabernacles are the bodies of the saints, which will once again be
erected and inhabited.[49] Still on the first day, the judgment seat of Christ
will take place.[50]

Because Methodius' view of the true meaning of this feast may be
esoteric to some readers, a brief explanation is here provided: The feasts
of Israel were shadows of great wonders that Jesus would perform (Col
2:16–17). The four spring feasts were all fulfilled by Jesus during his First
Coming on the very day they were celebrated, and in exact detail. The Mes-
siah fulfilled Passover (Lev 23:5) with his death on the cross (Rom 3:25),
Unleavened Bread (Lev 23:6) with his burial (John 6:35–51), Firstfruits
(Lev 23:9–11) with his resurrection (1 Cor 15:20), and Weeks or Pentecost
(Lev 23:15–16) with the Holy Spirit being sent in Jesus' name at Pentecost
(Acts 2:2–4). We are left to speculate as to what will fulfill the remaining
three fall feasts, though there is good evidence as to what each will be. The
Feast of Trumpets (Lev 23:23–25) is likely fulfilled by the resurrection and
the gathering together of those in Christ (1 Cor 15:51–52; 1 Thess 4:15–17).
The Day of Atonement (Lev 23:26–28) apparently foreshadows the Second
Coming (Zech 12:10–14; Matt 24:30–31; Rev 1:7).

The Feast of Tabernacles being fulfilled by the Millennium follows
both chronologically and scripturally. Jesus literally tabernacled with man
as the divine word housed in flesh (John 1:14).[51] He will tabernacle or live
among men on the earth once again (e.g., Isa 24:21–23; Zech 14:9; Rev
20:1–7). On the first day of Tabernacles, branches of olive, wild olive, myrtle, palm, and other leafy trees were gathered to make the tents (Lev 23:40;
Neh 8:15). At the triumphal entry, some in the crowd cut down branches to
spread on the road before Jesus (Matt 21:8). In like manner, saints coming
out of the great tribulation to enter the Millennium are described as holding palms in their hands (Rev 7:9–17). When Jesus previewed the kingdom

---

48. Ibid., 347. Methodius, *the Banquet of the Ten Virgins*, Discourse IX, Chapter V.

49. Ibid., 345. Methodius, *the Banquet of the Ten Virgins*, Discourse IX, Chapter III.

50. Ibid., 346. Methodius, *the Banquet of the Ten Virgins*, Discourse IX, Chapter III.

51. The Greek *skenoo* (skay-no'-o) is commonly translated as *dwelt* in John 1:14. It
literally means *to abide in a tabernacle*.

with his transfiguration, Peter offered to erect tents for him, Moses, and Elijah (Matt 17:1–4). The apostle directly associated the Messianic Age with the Feast of Tabernacles.

Zechariah 14 prophesies the Second Coming (v. 4) and subsequent events that take place during the Millennium. Only one feast is mentioned as being celebrated: Tabernacles. During the Messianic Age there will still be unbelievers on the earth. They will be forced to celebrate the Feast of Tabernacles or King Jesus will not allow rain to fall on their land (vv. 17–18). The importance of observing the feast during this time among even the unsaved is striking, for it was originally given only to the people of Israel (Lev 23:33–34, 42–43). Tabernacles was to be followed by a separate but related celebration: the eighth day assembly (Lev 23:36). The ante-Nicene fathers who identified the eighth day, following the seventh-day millennium, as the Eternal State may have found support in this post-Tabernacles observance. The relationship between the Feast of Tabernacles and the future earthly reign of Jesus is remarkable.

Methodius continued with what follows the millennial feast:

> Then again from thence I, a follower of Jesus, "who hath entered into the heavens," as they also, after the rest of the Feast of Tabernacles, come into the heavens, not continuing to remain in tabernacles—that is, my body after the space of a thousand years, changed from a human and corruptible form into angelic size and beauty, where at last we virgins, when the festival of the resurrection is consummated, shall pass from the wonderful place of the tabernacle to greater and better things, ascending into the very house of God above the heavens[52]

As a disciple of Jesus, Methodius saw himself as entering Heaven with a new angelic body after the thousand-year Feast of Tabernacles. In this respect, he took after Tertullian in teaching that Matthew 22:30 and Luke 20:36 occur after the Millennium and that the Eternal State will be in Heaven instead of on a new earth.

LACTANTIUS

Lucius Caelius Firmianus Lactantius was a theologian and the spiritual advisor to Constantine I. He helped shape some of the emperor's theology and

---

52. Ibid., 347. Methodius, *the Banquet of the Ten Virgins*, Discourse IX, Chapter V.

even tutored his son Crispus.[53] The father may have been given the name *Lactantius* due to the milky softness of his skin. He was a master of rhetoric, achieving far greater fame than his teacher Arnobius.[54] Lactantius' style was of such clarity, elegance, and dignity that he was known as the Christian Cicero.[55] His cardinal work, *the Divine Institutes*, is the first example of a systematic theology. He lived from about 240 to about 325 AD, the same year in which the First Council of Nicaea convened. How fitting it is, then, that the church father who represents the end of the ante-Nicene period strongly held to Premillennialism.

Lactantius' summary of future events opens with the observation that there is a superabundance of biblical data on the subject:

> *These are the things which are spoken of by the prophets as about to happen hereafter: but I have not considered it necessary to bring forward their testimonies and words, since it would be an endless task; nor would the limits of my book receive so great a multitude of subjects, since so many with one breath speak similar things . . . But he who wishes to know these things more accurately may draw from the fountain itself, and he will know more things worthy of admiration than we have comprised in these books. Perhaps some one may now ask when these things of which we have spoken are about to come to pass? I have already shown above, that when six thousand years shall be completed this change must take place*[56]

Lactantius' reluctance to provide exegesis on everything the prophets had to write concerning the coming kingdom speaks to the vast breadth of information available. After all, this is a man who provided extensive treatment on all other major areas of theology throughout his writings. And Lactantius had already written more than many theologians had concerning the end times in earlier chapters. After following his advice to read all the prophets, the student may wonder where to place so many of their glorious prophecies which have not yet come to pass. The father revealed that they will come about after the six thousand years are over. This is a reference to the sexta-septamillennial construct, which Lactantius covered previously.[57] Thus, the prophecies will take place during the Millennium and after.

---

53. Roberts et al., *Ante-Nicene Fathers Volume VII*, 6.

54. Ibid., 5.

55. Ibid., 7.

56. Ibid., 220. Lactantius, *the Divine Institutes*, Book VII, Chapter XXV.

57. Ibid., 211–212. Lactantius, *the Divine Institutes*, Book VII, Chapter XIV.

Ecology

Many of the prophecies are concerned with the future state of man, animals, and the environment. Lactantius connected these with the overall theme of Edenic conditions being restored:

> And as then a mortal and imperfect man was formed from the earth, that he might live a thousand years in this world; so now from this earthly age is formed a perfect man, that being quickened by God, he may bear rule in this same world through a thousand years.[58]

Like Justin Martyr, Lactantius understood that the Millennium will demonstrate that the sin and death of Adam during the first thousand years has been overcome. In the same world where an imperfect man failed, men made perfect by God will not only succeed in living for a thousand years, but will do so as rulers.

The heavens and the earth are to be freed from darkness and return to their former state:

> the moon will receive the brightness of the sun . . . but the sun will become seven times brighter than it now is; and the earth will open its fruitfulness, and bring forth most abundant fruits of its own accord; the rocky mountains shall drop with honey; streams of wine shall run down, and rivers flow with milk: in short, the world itself shall rejoice, and all nature exult, being rescued and set free from the dominion of evil and impiety, and guilt and error.[59]

Lactantius envisioned an augmented world where the production of fruit will reach astonishing levels. He partially quoted Joel 3:18, adding that the mountains will also drip honey. The description of the Promised Land flowing with milk and honey (Exod 3:8; Ezek 20:15) was seen as having world-wide application in the Millennium. This is the result of creation celebrating its freedom from sin.

Lactantius continued with what this means for animals:

> Throughout this time beasts shall not be nourished by blood, nor birds by prey; but all things shall be peaceful and tranquil. Lions and calves shall stand together at the manger, the wolf shall not carry off

---

58. Ibid., 212. Lactantius, *the Divine Institutes*, Book VII, Chapter XIV.
59. Ibid., 219. Lactantius, *the Divine Institutes*, Book VII, Chapter XXIV.

the sheep, the hound shall not hunt for prey; hawks and eagles shall not injure; the infant shall play with serpents.[60]

Isaiah 11:6–9 is among the most commonly cited millennial passages. Lactantius was just one more significant Christian leader that understood it to have a literal meaning.

Satan Imprisoned and Saints Reigning

Lactantius' Premillennialism was especially focused on the future binding of Satan and the rule of the saints:

> *We have said, a little before, that it will come to pass at the commencement of the sacred reign, that the prince of the devils will be bound by God. But he also, when the thousand years of the kingdom, that is, seven thousand of the world, shall begin to be ended, will be loosed afresh, and being sent forth from prison, will go forth and assemble all the nations, which shall then be under the dominion of the righteous, that they may make war against the holy city . . . Then the last anger of God shall come upon the nations, and shall utterly destroy them*[61]

Here we are introduced to Lactantius' novel name for the Millennium: *the sacred reign*. This period is distinctly identified as the kingdom, lasting for one thousand years. The Millennial Kingdom will commence with the binding of Satan. During which time the nations will be under the governmental authority of the saints. It is only at the end of the Millennium that Satan will be freed to gather an army to come against Jerusalem. He and his army will then be devoured by God's wrath. In short, Lactantius affirmed the plain meaning of Revelation 20:1–10.

In another chapter, Lactantius expanded with:

> *Then they who shall be alive in their bodies shall not die, but during those thousand years shall produce an infinite multitude, and their offspring shall be holy, and beloved by God; but they who shall be raised from the dead shall preside over the living as judges. But the nations shall not be entirely extinguished, but some shall be left as a victory for God, that they may be the occasion of triumph to the righteous, and may be subjected to perpetual slavery. About the same time also the prince of the devils, who is the contriver of all*

60. Ibid., 219. Lactantius, *the Divine Institutes*, Book VII, Chapter XXIV.
61. Ibid., 220. Lactantius, *the Divine Institutes*, Book VII, Chapter XXVI.

evils, shall be bound with chains, and shall be imprisoned during the thousand years of the heavenly rule in which righteousness shall reign in the world, so that he may contrive no evil against the people of God. After His coming the righteous shall be collected from all the earth, and the judgment being completed, the sacred city shall be planted in the middle of the earth, in which God Himself the builder may dwell together with the righteous, bearing rule in it.[62]

Lactantius wrote that after a period of great tribulation, Jesus would descend and judge the Antichrist and destroy his forces.[63] However, here we see that Lactantius held that some unbelievers would survive God's wrath to enter into the Millennium. The purpose for which is so that the saints will have a people to exercise their authority over. Satan being bound is not just incidental, but allows for the righteous to reign without having to contend with the Devil's influence over the world. Jerusalem will be the capital of the world, from where Jesus will live among his saints.

Though the saints will have great authority, it is Jesus who rules over all:

Therefore men will live a most tranquil life, abounding with resources, and will reign together with God; and the kings of the nations shall come from the ends of the earth with gifts and offerings, to adore and honour the great King, whose name shall be renowned and venerated by all the nations which shall be under heaven, and by the kings who shall rule on earth.[64]

The Final Resurrection

The father concluded with what is to take place after the Millennium, including the vital resurrection of the unjust:

But when the thousand years shall be completed, the world shall be renewed by God, and the heavens shall be folded together, and the earth shall be changed, and God shall transform men into the similitude of angels, and they shall be white as snow; and they shall always be employed in the sight of the Almighty, and shall make offerings to their Lord, and serve Him for ever. At the same time shall take place

---

62. Ibid., 219. Lactantius, *the Divine Institutes*, Book VII, Chapter XXIV.

63. Ibid., 215. Lactantius, *the Divine Institutes*, Book VII, Chapter XIX.

64. Ibid., 220. Lactantius, *the Divine Institutes*, Book VII, Chapter XXIV.

that second and public resurrection of all, in which the unrighteous shall be raised to everlasting punishments.[65]

Lactantius also took after Tertullian in teaching that the saints would receive angelic bodies only after the Millennium. However, unlike Tertullian and Methodius, Lactantius understood the Eternal State to be on a renewed earth and not in Heaven. Also taking place just after the Millennium is a second resurrection. Those partaking in this resurrection will be raised only to face eternal punishment for their sins, joining Satan and his servants in perpetual fire.[66] Lactantius interpreted Revelation 20:4–6 and 20:10–15 in a way that results from a natural reading. If there is no earthly millennial reign of Jesus then there should not be two different resurrections of the dead, bookending the thousand years. This is why opponents of Premillennialism typically believe in only one general resurrection of the dead. In affirming a final resurrection of the dead after the Millennium, Lactantius was strongly advocating Premillennialism. The editors of *the Ante-Nicene Fathers* noted that this point *clearly proves that the better sort of Chiliasm was not extinct in the Church.*[67]

PREMILLENNIALISM SPREAD THE GOSPEL

If space permitted we could consider the Premillennialism of other important fathers such as Hippolytus, Cyprian, Nepos, Victorinus, and many more. Even so, what is provided is surely enough to make all but the most biased concede that an anticipation of a coming millennial reign of Jesus was foundational in the early church. Even if the ante-Nicene church somehow misunderstood their teachers, the apostles, on such a significant issue as the coming kingdom, the premillennial belief had the virtue of helping to spread the Gospel.

The historian Adolf Harnack was critical of Premillennialism and nevertheless wrote the following:

First in point of time came the faith in the nearness of Christ's second advent and the establishing of His reign of glory on the earth. Indeed it appears so early that it might be questioned whether it ought not to be regarded as an essential part of the Christian religion . . . it

65. Ibid., 221. Lactantius, *the Divine Institutes*, Book VII, Chapter XXVI.
66. Ibid., 221. Lactantius, *the Divine Institutes*, Book VII, Chapter XXVI.
67. Ibid., 221.

must be admitted that this expectation was a prominent feature in the earliest proclamation of the gospel, and materially contributed to its success.[68]

J.C.I. Gieseler, another respected church historian, echoed Harnack in teaching that in *all these works the belief in the Millennium is so evident, that no one can hesitate to consider it as universal in an age, when certainly such motives as it offered were not unnecessary to animate men to suffer for Christianity.*[69] The hope placed in the coming millennial kingdom emboldened the early church to suffer persecution for the sake of the Gospel. Surely this is something that every believer can celebrate.

68. Harnack, "Millennium," 314–315.
69. Gieseler, *Ecclesiastical History Volume I*, 100.

10

Falling Away

THE DEATH OF LACTANTIUS in AD 325 marked the end of Premillennialism as a commonly held belief in the church until after the Reformation of the 16th century. No doubt there were some saints that read the Scriptures and believed what they said on the Messianic Age, though extant teachings on the matter are few. Even before the fourth century there were teachings against Premillennialism. However, these were undeveloped, with the critics typically demeaning many prophetic accounts, and in some instances even removing Revelation from their canons. *So early as the year 170, a church party in Asia Minor—the so-called Alogi—rejected the whole body of apocalyptic writings and denounced the Apocalypse of John as a book of fables.*[1] Most groups are not so honest in their rejection of the plain reading of Scripture. Others claim to view Revelation and other prophetic writings in the Bible as inspired by God. However, the normal meanings of these prophecies are often obfuscated or ignored in favor of uncovering some hidden meaning. These secret meanings are often so foreign to the text that the original audience would never have arrived at them.

ORIGEN AND ALLEGORY

The method of interpreting Scripture in this way is known as the allegorical hermeneutic. It was first promoted and largely developed by Origen at the turn of the third century. Origen (185–254 AD) was steeped in Greek philosophy, a perspective which greatly influenced his approach in

---

1. Harnack, "Millennium," 316.

understanding Scripture. This necessitated a militancy against Premillennialism. For Greek Philosophy typically viewed matter as being flawed, or even evil, while the nonphysical part of reality was good. Only a nonphysical and purely spiritual kingdom was acceptable to Origen and those in agreement with his Alexandrian theology. Origen provided no unified alternative to the many prophecies on the future earthly reign of the Messiah as a system. Instead, various passages on the matter were each relegated to having vague "spiritual" meanings, if they were addressed at all.

It is difficult to overestimate the level of influence Origen and his allegorical hermeneutic had in shaping much of the Christian world's approach to Scripture. One of his students, Dionysius, strongly opposed the promotion of Premillennialism through exegesis by the Egyptian church bishop Nepos. On what followed, Harnack recounted:

> *Dionysius became convinced that the victory of mystical theology over "Jewish" chiliasm would never be secure so long as the Apocalypse of John passed for an apostolic writing and kept its place among the homologoumena of the canon . . . In the course of the 4th century it was removed from the Greek canon, and thus the troublesome foundation on which chiliasm might have continued to build was got rid of . . . late in the Middle Ages, the Book of Revelation—by what means we cannot tell—did recover its authority, the church was by that time so hopelessly trammelled by a magical cultus as to be incapable of fresh developments.[2]*

MORE REASONS

Harnack's explanation reveals that Dionysius was also motivated by a distaste for Judaism. Theologian Renald Showers elaborated on the influence of anti-Semitism:

> *Gentiles who professed to be Christians increasingly called Jews "Christ-killers" and developed a strong bias against anything Jewish. Because the premillennial belief in the earthly, political Kingdom rule of Messiah in the future was the same hope which had motivated the Jews for centuries, that belief was increasingly "stigmatized as 'Jewish' and consequently 'heretical'" by eastern Gentile Christians.[3]*

2. Ibid.

3. Showers, *There Really is a Difference!*, 128.

Some of the same people who claimed to worship a Jew as God in the flesh, and hold up the Scriptures that were written by Jews (cf. Rom 3:1–2), were at the same time eager to separate themselves from what was Jewish. What absurdity! Unfortunately, this attitude is still commonplace in much of the Christian world to various degrees. The disassociation of the Bible from its Jewish context, background, and authorship has led to systemic deficits and blind spots in all areas of Christian theology. The very fact that the people the Tanakh was originally written to understood it to teach a literal and earthly reign of the Messiah is a strong reason to share in that expectation. It is true that most of the Jewish leadership in Jesus' day rejected him. But this is not because they believed in the Scriptures too much. Rather, they did not believe in what was written (cf. John 5:46–47).

Showers listed three other primary reasons for the rejection of Premillennialism in the early church. First, the Montanists, a sect of Christians often deemed as heretical, happened to include Chiliasm among their doctrines. Premillennialism predated Montanism and was established orthodox eschatology, but still unfairly suffered from the guilt by association fallacy. Second, some believers feared that the Romans would increase their persecution of the church if it was taught that Jesus would return and destroy their empire. Third, a few were concerned that the focus on the return of Jesus to reign on the earth diverted attention away from the daily work of the church.[4] None of these reasons are based upon the responsible exegesis of Scripture. The veracity of any doctrine must be determined by Scripture alone.

More detailed information on these issues can be studied in the following three works: an entry by Adolf Harnack, entitled "Millennium," found in the 1901 edition of *The Encyclopaedia Britannica*; in Philip Schaff's, *History of the Christian Church*; and in Renald Showers', *There Really is a Difference! A Comparison of Covenant and Dispensational Theology.*[5]

AUGUSTINE

Augustine was the bishop of Hippo, living from AD 354 to 430. He remains a vaunted theologian, having had a profound influence on Christianity in the West in his day and later on Roman Catholics and Protestants alike. Augustine serves as the cardinal figure in the turning away from

4. Ibid., 127–128.

5. The Harnack and Schaff works are available free of charge in Google Books.

Premillennialism. He once held to the doctrine before formulating the first truly developed alternative.

In *The City of God*, the bishop wrote on his transition:

> *There should follow on the completion of six thousand years, as of six days, a kind of seventh-day Sabbath in the succeeding thousand years; and that it is for this purpose the saints rise, viz., to celebrate this Sabbath. This opinion would not be objectionable, if it were believed that the joys of the saints in that Sabbath shall be spiritual, and consequent on the presence of God; for I myself, too, once held this opinion. But, as they assert that those who then rise again shall enjoy the leisure of immoderate carnal banquets, furnished with an amount of meat and drink such as not only to shock the feeling of the temperate, but even to surpass the measure of credulity itself, such assertions can only be believed by the carnal. They who do believe them are called by the spiritual Chiliasts, which we may literally reproduce by the name Millenarians.*[6]

Augustine refuted an argument never put forward by his opponents, a straw man fallacy. Premillennialists, whether in the early centuries or now, did and do believe that the joys in the Millennium are spiritual. They are, however, not only spiritual. And these blessings are certainly contingent upon God's presence. Augustine insulted Premillennialists for anticipating the enjoyment of food and drink. This is an unfair characterization. Such an expectation is not based on carnal desire, but on the plain reading of several prophetic passages, including Isaiah 25:6 and Matthew 26:29.

The quote is especially instructive in revealing Augustine's worldview. His disdain for what is physical suggests that his years of studying Greek philosophy had a lasting influence. Additionally, Augustine had once lived a life of hedonistic pleasure before converting to Christianity and becoming an ascetic. Perhaps he projected this life experience onto the Bible before interpreting it. Lest anyone think that Augustine's tendency to spiritualize Scripture was limited to prophecy, be assured that is not the case. He started doing so at the very beginning of Genesis. *Augustine early developed a spiritual exegesis of the creation story, affirming that "reproduce and multiply" (Gen. 1:27–28) meant a "spiritual reproduction" when the command was first given, not a physical production of offspring (Gn. adv. Man. 1.19.30).*[7]

6. Augustine, *City of God*, 785. Chapter VII.

7. Fitzgerald, *Augustine Through the Ages*, 69.

Augustine's Alternative

After declining to refute Premillennialism on each point, Augustine proceeded to show how he believed Revelation 20:1–7 should be understood. He put forth two possibilities as to the meaning of the one thousand years. First, it could refer to the final millennium before Jesus returns to set up his eternal kingdom. This option takes the length of time literally but applies it to the end of the present age. Second, the thousand years could refer to the entire duration of the world, representing the perfected fullness of time. It is perfect in that one thousand is ten cubed. Furthermore, the number one hundred is said to indicate totality. This is based on Jesus' teaching in Mark 10:30 that sacrificial servants will receive a hundred times what they left behind. And in the number one thousand there are ten hundreds.[8]

Augustine placed the binding and imprisonment of Satan for the thousand years in the present age. He identified the chain as a restraining force that prevents the Devil from gaining possession of believers.[9] The abyss that the angel throws Satan into is said to represent *the countless multitude of the wicked whose hearts are unfathomably deep in malignity against the Church of God.*[10]

On the rule of Jesus and his saints:

> But while the Devil is bound, the saints reign with Christ during the same thousand years, understood in the same way, that is, of the time of His first coming . . . the Church could not now be called His kingdom or the kingdom of heaven unless His saints were even now reigning with Him, though in another and far different way; for to His saints He says, "Lo, I am with you always, even to the end of the world."[11]

The church is essentially made to be one and the same as the kingdom. Since it is virtually impossible to argue that the saints are now reigning according to the regular sense, Augustine had to find another one. The fact that Jesus remains with the saints is taken to mean that they are currently reigning with him.

Augustine agreed with Premillennialism in taking the second resurrection literally and in placing it at the end of the thousand years. He

8. Augustine, 785–786. Chapter VII.
9. Ibid., 786. Chapter VII.
10. Ibid., 786. Chapter VII.
11. Ibid., 790. Chapter IX.

differed in interpreting the first resurrection to indicate those who have been revived from the death of sin and continue in a renewed life.[12]

These interpretations on the thousand years, the binding of Satan, the reign of the saints, and the first resurrection provided the basis for what came to be known as Amillennialism.

AMILLENNIALISM

Amillennialism is the name for the view that there is no literal and earthly reign of Jesus before the Eternal State. When the prefix *a* is attached to the beginning of a word it negates the meaning. Thus, Amillennialism means *no millennium*. In general, amillennialists contend that the rule of the saints, as depicted in Revelation 20, with Christ is only spiritual. It started with the First Coming and will end with the Second. The present age, is then, the thousand year kingdom; the number is only symbolic or spiritual. Satan is now bound in that his power is limited in some sense. The first resurrection of the dead is considered to be a synonym for the regeneration and/or salvation of the believer. Finally, many of the promises made in the unconditional covenants to Israel are considered fulfilled or as currently being fulfilled with the Christian church. Notably, Jesus is viewed as presently sitting on the throne of David, though in heaven and not on earth.[13]

Amillennialists utilize a hermeneutic that allows for spiritual or non-literal interpretations of unfulfilled prophecy. This is despite the fact that they strongly affirm the literal fulfillment of a great many prophecies with the First Coming. On the need to be consistent in interpreting First and Second Coming prophecies, the evangelical-champion J.C. Ryle wrote:

> As He came the first time in person, so He will come the second time in person. As He went away from earth visibly, so He will return visibly. As He literally rode upon an ass, was literally sold for thirty pieces of silver, had His hands and feet literally pierced, was numbered literally with the transgressors, and had lots literally cast upon His raiment, and all that Scripture might be fulfilled, so also will He literally come, literally set up a kingdom, and literally reign over the earth, because the very same Scripture has said that it shall be so.[14]

12. Ibid., 793. Chapter IX.

13. Some premillennialists also hold this view. However, they still anticipate a future reign of Jesus upon the earth.

14. Ryle, *Coming Events*, 14.

Such a dedication to the consistent literal interpretation of prophecy underscores the primary deficit in where the amillennialists are coming from. Yes, their views can be responded to on a point by point basis. However, the issue on who is correct will always revert back to what method of approaching God's word allows for him to have the final say.

Response

The best refutation of a position often comes from providing the better option. This has been the desired goal and focus in writing on the Millennium throughout this book. Therefore, just a few general responses to Amillennialism are provided. First, whether or not the thousand years is a set number or just representative of a specific period is not the primary issue. The premillennial position is based on an intermediary period where covenantal promises to Israel can be fulfilled and a great number of prophecies can find a home. Even if the amillennialist is correct in claiming that the number of years is symbolic or spiritual, the underlying basis for Premillennialism remains untouched. Questioning the literalness of the thousand years is merely a tactic used to obfuscate and avoid the far more significant scriptural basis for Premillennialism.

That the blessed Thousand years are not yet begun, is abundantly clear from this, we do not see the Devil bound; No, the Devil was never more let loose than in our days.[15] This observation by the Puritan Cotton Mather is strongly supported by several New Testament passages. Jesus explained that Satan was a murderer, the father of lies (John 8:44), and the ruler of the world (John 14:30). Well after the ascension of Jesus, Paul referred to Satan as the god of this world (2 Cor 4:4). The apostle further described Satan as the prince of the power of the air and the spirit that is now working in the sons of disobedience (Eph 2:2), as an active tempter (1 Thess 3:5). James instructed the early church to resist the Devil (Jas 4:7). Peter warned his brethren that they should be on alert, for their adversary the Devil prowls around like a roaring lion, looking for someone to devour (1 Pet 5:8). Satan was such a present danger to the churches of Revelation 2–3 that he is mentioned six times, as both a direct and indirect persecutor (Rev 2:9, 10, 13, 24; 3:9). Without a doubt, Scripture depicts Satan as an unchained menace that the saints must oppose. Moreover, the abyss that Satan is to be thrown into was spoken of as a real place where demons are afraid to

15. Mather and Mather, *Wonders of the Invisible World*, 69.

go (Luke 8:31). The abyss is not said to represent the hearts of the wicked or anything else that would allow for the conclusion that Satan is currently imprisoned there.

In an effort to support the notion that the first resurrection of Revelation 20:5–6 is not of the body, amillennialists look to John 5. Jesus did in fact refer to those who are saved as having passed out of death into life (John 5:24). Jesus specifically defined what is meant by this "resurrection." The first resurrection of Revelation 20 is never given any special definition that would make it mean something other than what it usually would. Jesus also spoke of a time coming when all in their tombs will hear his voice. Some will be resurrected to life, while others will be resurrected to face judgment (John 5:28–29). The amillennialist takes these resurrections as referring to two classes of people within an overall one-time raising of the dead at the end of the age. Nothing in the plain reading of Revelation 20 contradicts John 5. Jesus' purpose was not to provide an eschatological timetable, but rather to teach on his authority as it applied to the areas of resurrection and judgment (vv. 21–27). The point, then, is that both the just and unjust will be resurrected for different purposes. Jesus never said that both groups would be resurrected together.

In the normal use of language, the same word used in the same context maintains its meaning. If one resurrection in Revelation 20:5–6 is of the body, then so is the other. Additionally, the two resurrections are used as bookends to the Millennium. If the first resurrection meant salvation, then why is it placed only at the beginning of the Millennium? Is it not the case that people are saved throughout the present age?

THE REFORMATION

Augustine's influence was so dominant that Amillennialism went largely unchallenged until well into the Reformation. On why Premillennialism did not make an immediate return at that time, John MacArthur explained:

> *The Reformers had it right on most issues. But they never got around to eschatology. They never got around to applying their formidable skills. You cannot fight the war on every front. And at the great time of the Reformation, they were fighting the war where the battle raged the hottest and that was over the gospel and over the nature of Christ and over salvation by grace through faith and over the authority of Scripture. They were fighting the massive Roman system. And being*

occupied on those fronts, they never really got to the front of escha-
tology . . . [16]

This does not mean that the Reformers held to no eschatological position at all. It means that their high view of God's word over the traditions of men was not seriously applied to what was a lower priority. This resulted in a lingering Amillennialism.

John Calvin's remarks are emblematic:

> But a little later there followed the chiliasts, who limited the reign of Christ to a thousand years. Now their fiction is too childish either to need or to be worth a refutation. And the Apocalypse, from which they undoubtedly drew a pretext for their error, does not support them. For the number 'one thousand' [Rev. 20:4] does not apply to the eternal blessedness of the church but only to the various disturbances that awaited the church, while still toiling on earth. On the contrary, all Scripture proclaims that there will be no end to the blessedness of the elect or the punishment of the wicked [Matt. 25:41, 46].[17]

It is rather difficult to find more than a few pages in a row from Calvin's *Institutes of the Christian Religion* that lack a reference to Augustine. Such was the level of influence Augustine held over the reformer. Calvin even followed after Augustine in mischaracterizing the beliefs of the chiliasts or early premillennialists. If these fathers really believed that the reign of Christ would come to an end after the Millennium then they deserved to be mocked. Of course this is not what the chiliasts believed, nor is it even a remotely accurate description of Premillennialism in general. The reign of Jesus does not end with the Millennium. He will remain King on the new earth for all eternity. Blessings upon the saints and punishments upon the wicked will last just as long.

And what of Calvin's brief explanation as to the meaning of the thousand years? The church facing disturbances while toiling on the earth is almost the opposite of reigning alongside King Jesus. Calvin was an exegetical genius on many biblical subjects. Unfortunately, he did not put the same effort into seriously unpacking the Scriptures when it came to the Millennium. Calvin wrote a commentary on nearly every book of the Bible, but Revelation was not among them. *Now frankly it's too late for John Calvin*

---

16. MacArthur, "Why Every Calvinist Should Be a Premillennialist, Part 1," lines 90–96.

17. Calvin, *Institutes of the Christian Religion*, 995. Book III, Chapter XXV, Number V.

to fix his work, although he is now a premillennialist in heaven. If only he could just send down one message, that might be it.[18]

JOSEPH MEDE

Joseph Mede (1586–1639) is one of the most fascinating figures from the twilight of the Reformation. He was not only a widely influential church scholar, but also a naturalist and Egyptologist. Mede was well schooled in biblical languages, subjects he lectured on at Christ's College of the University of Cambridge. Mede broke with his contemporaries in returning to the literal interpretation of the prophetic Scriptures. His book, *The Key of the Revelation,* was a clarion call for a return to Premillennialism. *Mede was certain that the thousand years of the millennium . . . represented the future reign of the saints with Christ . . . Mede Identified the millennium with the future seventh trumpet and the day of judgment, both of which, he argued, would last one thousand years. It was a systematic repudiation of the Reformer's Augustinianism.*[19]

Mede was a harbinger; after him came the flood. William Twisse, Prolocutor of the Westminster Assembly, wrote a preface to the 1643 English translation of *The Key of Revelation.* In it, he rebuked Augustine for relinquishing the doctrine of Christ's Kingdom on earth and praised Mede for returning to it.[20] Isaac Newton, arguably the most prolific scientist in history, acknowledged Mede as the greatest influence on his interpretation of biblical prophecy.[21] The list of church leaders and Bible scholars following Mede in becoming premillennialists continues at some length.

POSTMILLENNIALISM

In the late 17th century, the Unitarian Daniel Whitby (1638–1726) developed a new alternative to both Premillennialism and Amillennialism: Postmillennialism.[22] Just as the name suggests, Postmillennialism is the belief that Jesus will return after the thousand years of Revelation 20. In

18. MacArthur. Lines 218–219.
19. Gribben, *Puritan Millennium,* 43–44.
20. Ibid., 44.
21. Iliffe, "Newton's Life and Work at a Glance," lines 76–81.
22. Pate, *Reading Revelation,* 8.

this scheme, the Millennium, whether literal or figurative for a long period, is a golden age where Christianity has conquered the unbelieving world. During this time most, if not all, people will become saved and biblical values will flourish. This will so move Jesus that he will return, resurrect the dead all at once, and inaugurate the Eternal State. The Millennial Kingdom is one brought about by the efforts of man instead of by the Messiah upon his return. Postmillennialism is a version of Amillennialism in that it too denies the literal reign of Jesus upon the earth during the thousand years.

There are differing opinions among postmillennialists as to both the nature and extent of the positive changes that must occur. Among conservative postmillennialists, the more important emphasis is placed on the going forth of the Gospel and those saved by hearing it. Many of them also include advances in science, medicine, and human governments in contributing to the improvement of the present age. Another point of disagreement is on how many people will become saved during this golden age. The majority opinion has been that a great many will be saved, without being more specific. While fewer in number, influential postmillennialists, such as B.B. Warfield and Heinrich A.W. Meyer, have argued that every single person alive will become a believer before Jesus returns.

On the key points in Revelation 20, Kenneth Gentry summarized his postmillennial beliefs:

> This binding does not result in the total inactivity of Satan; rather it restrains his power by Christ's superior might . . . In Revelation 20:4–6 we see the positive implications of Christ's Kingdom. While Satan is bound, Christ rules and His redeemed people participate with Him in that rule (Rev. 20:4). These participants include both the quick and the dead: the martyred saints in heaven ("those who had been beheaded because of the testimony of Jesus and because of the word of God") and the persevering saints on earth ("and those who [Gk: oitines] had not worshiped the beast") (NASB). Christ's kingdom rule involves all those who suffer for Him and enter heaven above, as well as those who live for Him during their earthly sojourn.[23]

---

23. Gentry, "The Meaning of the "Millennium"," lines 84–97.

Response

Again, this book's focus is not on refuting positions in conflict with Premillennialism. Therefore, only some general remarks are provided. First, to claim that the binding of Satan means that his power has merely been limited is unconvincing. The picture painted by Revelation 20:1–3 is of an angel wrapping a great chain around the ancient serpent, casting him into the abyss and sealing it over him (cf. Luke 8:31). This is the outright imprisonment of Satan, not merely a stifling of his influence as he roams free. The purpose of the Devil's confinement is so that he can no longer gain access to the nations to deceive them (Rev 20:3). Surely Satan is not restricted from doing so in the present age (e.g., John 14:30; 2 Cor 4:4; 1 Pet 5:8). The same criticisms made on the amillennial interpretation of the binding apply here as well.

Note that the reign of the saints with Christ is defined as suffering and living for him. To reign is to have great authority, akin to a sovereign. The actual meaning of the word is antithetical to what the postmillennialist would have us believe. Revelation 20:4–6 is clear in teaching that the saints rule with Christ after they are brought to life. The reign does not include those in heaven, a location the passage makes no mention of. Indeed, the apostle previously wrote that the reign of the saints will take place upon the earth (Rev 5:10).

Over the centuries it should be expected that broader eschatological beliefs would become more specific and systematized, complete with variations according to different interpretations. It is quite another matter to posit an entirely new doctrine on the Millennium over 1,500 years after the close of the Canon. It is fair for the postmillennialist to find some points of agreement in Augustine's Amillennialism. However, the expectation that the world will become progressively better before the return of Jesus is the opposite of what the early church held to. According to Lactantius, *as the end of the world approaches the condition of human affairs must undergo a change, and through the prevalence of wickedness become worse; so that now these times of ours, in which iniquity and impiety have increased even to the highest degree, may be judged happy and almost golden in comparison of that incurable evil.*[24]

---

24. Roberts et al., *Ante-Nicene Fathers Volume VII*, 212. Lactantius, *the Divine Institutes*, Book VII, Chapter XV.

Lactantius, and the early Christian leaders he represents, have a great deal of support in the overall thrust of Scripture. The kingdoms of fallen man will continue until they are suddenly crushed and replaced by the Messiah's kingdom at his coming (Dan 2:44–45). The sons of the evil one are to remain among the sons of the kingdom throughout the present age. Only when it ends will those who commit lawlessness be removed (Matt 13:24–30, 36–43). Just before the coming of Christ on the clouds, there will be a period of tribulation and then great tribulation such as has not occurred since the beginning of the world (Matt 24:4–30; cf. Rev 1:7). A litany of sins will continue to be practiced until the Second Coming (2 Tim 3:1–13; cf. 2 Tim 4:3–4). In the later times some will fall away from the faith, turning to deceitful spirits, and the doctrines of demons (1 Tim 4:1). Before the day of the Lord can come, there must first be an apostasy and the man of lawlessness revealed (2 Thess 2:1–4).

Charles Spurgeon:

> Paul does not paint the future with rose-colour: he is no smooth-tongued prophet of a golden age, into which this dull earth may be imagined to be glowing. There are sanguine brethren who are looking forward to everything growing better and better and better, until, at last, this present age ripens into a millennium. They will not be able to sustain their hopes, for Scripture gives them no solid basis to rest upon. We who believe that there will be no millennial reign without the King, and who expect no rule of righteousness except from the appearing of the righteous Lord, are nearer the mark. Apart from the second Advent of our Lord, the world is more likely to sink into a pandemonium than to rise into a millennium. A divine interposition seems to me the hope set before us in Scripture, and, indeed, to be the only hope adequate to the occasion.[25]

When the normal meaning of Scripture is ignored it is often due to some outside influence upon its readers. Postmillennialism was born out of the historical climate that was the end of the Renaissance. There was a general consensus that the world was improving through human efforts. This impression not only guided Whitby in formulating his eschatology, but lent to its adoption by others. During the 18th century Great Awakening in the United States, Postmillennialism naturally increased in popularity. Jonathan Edwards deserves much credit for shaping the mass revival. It is no accident that he remains the most erudite of the postmillennial theologians.

---

25. Spurgeon, "The Form of Godliness without the Power," 301.

Postmillennialism's popularity historically rises and falls along with positive and negative world events. If there is a long period of peace and revival, then Postmillennialism becomes easy to embrace. While if there is a world war or an increase in the persecution of Christians, then Postmillennialism quickly loses favor. No matter what view of the Millennium one holds to, its veracity must be determined by what Scripture says, not on the current perception of the world.

Postmillennialists often say that theirs is the eschatology of hope. Well, since premillennialists rely on the coming of Jesus to bring about the Millennium, theirs is the eschatology of the blessed hope (Titus 2:13).

HE WILL COME FIRST

All three major views on the Millennium are held today. Evangelicals are typically premillennial while Roman Catholics and mainline Protestants are typically amillennial. A minority of mainline Protestants and evangelicals are postmillennial. The overall thinking of this author echoes the words of Charles Spurgeon:

> If I read the word aright, and it is honest to admit that there is much room for difference of opinion here, the day will come, when the Lord Jesus will descend from heaven with a shout, with the trump of the archangel and the voice of God. Some think that this descent of the Lord will be post-millennial—that is, after the thousand years of his reign. I cannot think so. I conceive that the advent will be pre-millennial—that He will come first; and then will come the millennium as the result of his personal reign upon earth.[26]

26. Spurgeon, "Justification and Glory," 249.

11

Present Age, Millennium, or Eternal State?

PASSAGES ON THE MILLENNIUM are found regularly throughout Scripture, from Genesis to Revelation. Many fail to recognize this because a given writer did not explicitly mention a thousand year reign of the Messiah. This is not a problem, as the specificity of the thousand years in Revelation 20 is a product of progressive revelation. The transitional nature of the Millennium is more important, and it is this fact that was so often spoken of by the prophets. The vast amount of passages that describe the Millennium are determined through induction. This means that many promises and prophecies anticipate events or realities that could only fit in the Millennium. For various reasons, these types of passages could not rightly be understood to find their fulfillment in the present age or in the Eternal State. The following is a list of a tiny fraction of passages that find their home in the Millennium. Many of the most prominent are not included due to their treatment in previous chapters, though some are briefly referenced again. It is requested of the reader, that as you consider each passage, ask yourself if it best fits in the present age, in the Millennium, or in the Eternal State. The question is rhetorical, with the answer always being the same. The point of the exercise is to appreciate the inductive study of Scripture, as prophecy so often demands.

THE TORAH

The first five books of the Bible, penned by Moses, contain powerful narratives, charged with millennial implications. The first of two key passages considered here is Isaac's blessing of Jacob in Genesis 27:27–29:

> So he came near and kissed him. And Isaac smelled the smell of his garments and blessed him and said, "See, the smell of my son is as the smell of a field that the LORD has blessed! May God give you of the dew of heaven and of the fatness of the earth and plenty of grain and wine. Let peoples serve you, and nations bow down to you. Be lord over your brothers, and may your mother's sons bow down to you. Cursed be everyone who curses you, and blessed be everyone who blesses you!"

Jacob hardly enjoyed an abundance of food and wine provided especially for him; a great famine forced the patriarch to move to Egypt simply to survive (Gen 46–47). Peoples and nations never came to bow before Jacob and serve him. On the contrary, Jacob served Laban for twenty years (Gen 31:38). He later bowed before his brother Esau seven times (Gen 33:3), a tribute typically reserved for kings. Jacob died without ever receiving parts of the blessing that were owed to him. He must be resurrected in order to enjoy the fullness of the birthright. While the blessing will in many respects continue in the Eternal State, the aspect of nations bowing before Jacob begins when Israel is set above them (e.g., Isa 2:2–4). Indeed, the blessing has another application in gifts and honor being afforded to the nation that sprung from Jacob. Both applications are realized in the Millennium.

Next, is the related Deuteronomy 26:18–19:

> And the LORD has declared today that you are a people for his treasured possession, as he has promised you, and that you are to keep all his commandments, and that he will set you in praise and in fame and in honor high above all nations that he has made, and that you shall be a people holy to the LORD your God, as he promised."

This concludes a small section following the dispensing of the covenant law to the people as they were about to enter the Promised Land (Deut 5–26:15). Moses reminded them of their oath to follow the LORD and obey his commandments (Deut 26:16–17). Israel could not maintain fidelity and so the LORD was under no obligation to place Israel above all the other nations. Nevertheless, his evangelistic purpose for the nation was revealed (cf. Deut 28; Isa 60:1–3). Israel's ideal state was not and cannot be reached in the present age, for it will end with her national recognition that Jesus is Lord and Savior, prompting his return (e.g., Matt 23:39; Acts 3:19–21; Rom 11:25–27). When Israel is high and lifted up, nations and peoples will stream to Jerusalem to entreat the LORD and learn his ways (e.g., Isa 2:2–4; Mic 4:1–3; Zech 8:22–23). In the Eternal State, only those already written in the Lamb's book of life are allowed entry (Rev 21:27).

PSALMS

Psalm 2:4–6:

> He who sits in the heavens laughs; the Lord holds them in derision.
> Then he will speak to them in his wrath, and terrify them in his fury,
> saying, "As for me, I have set my King on Zion, my holy hill."

Psalm 2 is a great royal psalm on the rule of the messianic King. The nations will resolve to rebel against God and his Anointed, in an effort to unfetter themselves (vv. 1–3). The LORD will become amused with their efforts, for the Messiah will be reigning from Jerusalem. He has been given the nations as an inheritance, and will rule over them with a rod of iron (vv. 7–9). The rulers of the earth are counseled to worship the LORD and pay homage to the Son to avoid his wrath (vv. 10–12). Jesus would need to return in order to begin his rule from Jerusalem, meaning the passage cannot be fulfilled in the present age. In the Eternal State there will be none who rebel against the LORD and his Son.

Psalm 72:8–11:

> May he have dominion from sea to sea, and from the River to the
> ends of the earth! May desert tribes bow down before him, and his
> enemies lick the dust! May the kings of Tarshish and of the coast-
> lands render him tribute; may the kings of Sheba and Seba bring
> gifts! May all kings fall down before him, all nations serve him!

This passage reflects Solomon's desire for his own rule but finds its fulfill-ment in the Messiah's. The area of the Messiah's reign is to extend from the Euphrates to all over the world. When did all the kings of the earth come to prostrate themselves before the Davidic King? Our Lord did not receive the honor he deserved from his own people at the First Coming, let alone tribute from other nations. In the Eternal State, no enemies of the Messiah will be granted an audience.

Psalm 110:2:

The LORD sends forth from Zion your mighty scepter. Rule in the midst of your enemies!

Again, the messianic King will rule from Jerusalem and from there his authority will stretch forth. This did not happen at the First Coming and so must occur at the Second. Since the reign takes place in a world full of Jesus' enemies, it cannot be in the Eternal State.

ISAIAH

Isaiah contains far more millennial passages than any other book in Scripture, including some of the most descriptive and comprehensive. Following the classic depiction of the Millennium in Isaiah 11:6–9, is the instructive 11:10–12:

> *In that day the root of Jesse, who shall stand as a signal for the peoples—of him shall the nations inquire, and his resting place shall be glorious. In that day the Lord will extend his hand yet a second time to recover the remnant that remains of his people, from Assyria, from Egypt, from Pathros, from Cush, from Elam, from Shinar, from Hamath, and from the coastlands of the sea. He will raise a signal for the nations and will assemble the banished of Israel, and gather the dispersed of Judah from the four corners of the earth.*

The root of Jesse, the Messiah (cf. Isa 11:1; Rev 5:5; 22:16), will be sought by the nations. This is what we see in Isaiah 2:2–4, with the nations coming to Jerusalem to learn from the LORD. This cannot begin until after Jesus returns. The second ingathering of the Jewish people back to the Promised Land will occur at the Second Coming (Matt 24:30–31; cf. Isa 27:12–13). Furthermore, Jewish people coming from the coastlands of the sea does not fit in the Eternal State because there will be no more seas in that time (Rev 21:1).

Isaiah 19:24–25:

> *In that day Israel will be the third with Egypt and Assyria, a blessing in the midst of the earth, whom the LORD of hosts has blessed, saying, "Blessed be Egypt my people, and Assyria, the work of my hands, and Israel my inheritance."*

God actually referred to Egypt as *my people*! This is the position of intimacy that God often used of Israel in describing her as his own possession out of all the nations on the earth (e.g., Deut 7:6–8; 14:22; Ps 135:4; Isa 43:1–3; Jer

31:1–4; Ezek 36:28; Joel 3:1–2; Rom 11:2). Egypt and Assyria, once enemies of Israel, will become affixed to her as one commonwealth of God's people. This is truly incredible. The new relationship begins *in that day*, i.e., the day of the LORD, after the return of the Messiah (cf. Zech 14:4, 9). It cannot begin in the Eternal State; everyone on the new earth will be part of God's people. The contrast created by the three nations being set against the others is typical of millennial narratives.

Isaiah 24:21–23:

> On that day the LORD will punish the host of heaven, in heaven, and the kings of the earth, on the earth. They will be gathered together as prisoners in a pit; they will be shut up in a prison, and after many days they will be punished. Then the moon will be confounded and the sun ashamed, for the LORD of hosts reigns on Mount Zion and in Jerusalem, and his glory will be before his elders.

During the day of the LORD, he will separate the human authorities and the fallen angels from the world in order to cease their influence over it. The period of imprisonment will be for many days, with a final punishment to follow. This matches the description of Satan's imprisonment during the Millennium, eventually ending with him, the false prophet, the beast, and anyone's name not found in the book of life being cast into the lake of fire (Rev 20). Wicked rulers are myriad in the present age and Satan is free to roam about like a roaring lion, looking for people to devour (1 Pet 5:8). Since the period of many days is limited and ends with a judgment, it would hardly fit in the Eternal State when all final sentences have been handed down. Here, then, is a clear reference to a transitional period that can only indicate the Millennium.

Isaiah 56:6–7:

> "And the foreigners who join themselves to the LORD, to minister to him, to love the name of the LORD, and to be his servants, everyone who keeps the Sabbath and does not profane it, and holds fast my covenant—these I will bring to my holy mountain, and make them joyful in my house of prayer; their burnt offerings and their sacrifices will be accepted on my altar; for my house shall be called a house of prayer for all peoples."

Gentiles will be taken to Jerusalem's great mountain of Isaiah 2:2–4. They will be allowed to worship in the temple and to even offer sacrifices. This was never permitted in any of the previous temples, nor will it be in the final one of this age (Rev 11:1–2). There is no temple at all in the Eternal State

(Rev 21:22). The passage summarizes what will happen in the temple that is to be constructed under the supervision of the Messiah after he returns (Zech 6:12–13, 15; cf. Ezek 40–48).

Isaiah 60:12:

> For the nation and kingdom that will not serve you shall perish;
> those nations shall be utterly laid waste.

Isaiah 60 describes Israel and Jerusalem's future glory, with many of the verses signaling that they belong in the Millennium. Verse 12 is the most concise in this regard. Never before have the nations faced destruction for not serving Jerusalem, nor is this reasonable to expect before Jesus returns. It would be inconceivable for a nation to oppose God's directives in the Eternal State.

Isaiah 65:20:

> No more shall there be in it an infant who lives but a few days, or
> an old man who does not fill out his days, for the young man shall
> die a hundred years old, and the sinner a hundred years old shall be
> accursed.

Since the time Isaiah was given this revelation, when was a centenarian considered young? Moses said that the normal lifespan in his day was from seventy to eighty years (Ps 90:10). Even when this great extension in age becomes the norm, death will remain, along with the sin that leads to it. The passage does not describe the present age and cannot fit in the Eternal State, where there is no death (Rev 21:4).

DANIEL

Daniel 2:44 and 7:11–12:

> And in the days of those kings the God of heaven will set up a king-
> dom that shall never be destroyed, nor shall the kingdom be left to
> another people. It shall break in pieces all these kingdoms and bring
> them to an end, and it shall stand forever,

> "I looked then because of the sound of the great words that the horn
> was speaking. And as I looked, the beast was killed, and its body
> destroyed and given over to be burned with fire. As for the rest of
> the beasts, their dominion was taken away, but their lives were pro-
> longed for a season and a time.

The kingdom will suddenly come to destroy and replace the kingdoms of man (cf. Dan 2:34–35; 7:14, 27). At the beginning of God's eternal kingdom is a season, during which the peoples of man's kingdom are allowed to continue. This transitional period happens after Jesus returns to establish the Kingdom of God, but before the Eternal State, where there will be no remnants of man's kingdom (Rev 21:3).

MINOR PROPHETS

Zephaniah 3:9–20 is a noteworthy summary of the Millennium, with a focus on blessings for both Jew and Gentile. Verses 9–10:

> *"For at that time I will change the speech of the peoples to a pure speech, that all of them may call upon the name of the LORD and serve him with one accord. From beyond the rivers of Cush my worshipers, the daughter of my dispersed ones, shall bring my offering.*

The depiction of nations becoming unified in their worship of the LORD and pilgrimages being made to bring him offerings[1] matches several other millennial narratives (e.g., Ps 72:10). The account takes place after the LORD pours out his indignation on the kingdoms of the earth (Zeph 3:8), a future judgment. The Messiah will have returned, ruling as King of Israel in her midst (v. 15). At that time, Jesus will deal with Israel's oppressors (v. 19), a group that will not be present in the Eternal State.

Second only to Isaiah, Zechariah wrote more on the coming of the Messiah than did the other prophets. Many of these prophecies concerned the Second Coming and the Millennium. Zechariah 8:22–23:

> *Many peoples and strong nations shall come to seek the LORD of hosts in Jerusalem and to entreat the favor of the LORD. Thus says the LORD of hosts: In those days ten men from the nations of every tongue shall take hold of the robe of a Jew, saying, 'Let us go with you, for we have heard that God is with you.'"*

Jesus must return before all sorts of people groups and citizens of mighty nations will be able to travel to Jerusalem to seek his favor. In the Eternal State, everyone will be with God and will not require the help of others to find him. The desire to follow a Jew on his way to see the Messiah is

---

1. The offerings are the Jewish people themselves, escorted by Gentiles to the Promised Land.

indicative of the Millennium, when Israel is set above the nations that do not know the LORD.

Zechariah 14:8–9:

> On that day living waters shall flow out from Jerusalem, half of them to the eastern sea and half of them to the western sea. It shall continue in summer as in winter. And the LORD will be king over all the earth. On that day the LORD will be one and his name one.

Here is a companion passage that provides extra detail on the movement of the river that will flow from the millennial temple (cf. Ezek 47:1–12). The water will flow *on that day*, referring to the Second Coming of the Messiah a few verses before (Zech 14:4). Also on the day of his return, Jesus will be king over the entire earth, reigning as a singular monarch. The world to be ruled over is the current one on which he returns to, not the new one of the Eternal State (Rev 21:1).

Zechariah 14:16–19:

> Then everyone who survives of all the nations that have come against Jerusalem shall go up year after year to worship the King, the LORD of hosts, and to keep the Feast of Booths. And if any of the families of the earth do not go up to Jerusalem to worship the King, the LORD of hosts, there will be no rain on them. And if the family of Egypt does not go up and present themselves, then on them there shall be no rain; there shall be the plague with which the LORD afflicts the nations that do not go up to keep the Feast of Booths. This shall be the punishment to Egypt and the punishment to all the nations that do not go up to keep the Feast of Booths.

Again, this is part of a narrative that takes place after the Second Coming (Zech 14:4). The peoples of the earth will have to travel to Jerusalem to worship King Messiah and observe the Feast of Tabernacles. If they do not then they will be punished by the withholding of rain on their lands. In the present age, God sends rain on the righteous and the unrighteous alike (Matt 5:45). No threats will be needed to convince people to come and worship God in the Eternal State, for all will joyfully do so (Rev 21:3).

Malachi 3:2–4:

> But who can endure the day of his coming, and who can stand when he appears? For he is like a refiner's fire and like fullers' soap. He will sit as a refiner and purifier of silver, and he will purify the sons of Levi and refine them like gold and silver, and they will bring offerings in righteousness to the LORD. Then the offering of Judah and

Jerusalem will be pleasing to the LORD as in the days of old and as in former years.

It is the Second Coming that warrants the portrayal of Jesus as a purifying fire and the rhetorical question, *who can stand?* The passage conforms to the many others that tell of sacrifices offered in the millennial temple (e.g., Isa 56:6–8; Jer 33:14–18; Ezek 43:18–27; Zech 14:20–21). There is no death in the Eternal State (Rev 21:4), including animals.

THE NEW TESTAMENT

The majority of New Testament passages pertaining to the Millennium are those that teach on the kingdom, when Jesus returns to reign from his throne (Matt 25:31–34). One of the most striking is Matthew 8:11:

> *I tell you, many will come from east and west and recline at table with Abraham, Isaac, and Jacob in the kingdom of heaven,*

Before anyone can sit at a table with Abraham, Isaac, and Jacob, the fathers need to be resurrected in the coming kingdom. While the opportunity to spend time with the patriarchs will likely remain in the Eternal State, Gentiles traveling from around the world to visit them corresponds with previously considered millennial passages on Israel as a witness to the nations. Jesus was probably alluding to the coronation banquet he will prepare at the beginning of the Millennium, described in Isaiah 25:6–9 (cf. Isa 65:13–14; Matt 26:29).

Acts 15:16–18:

> *"'After this I will return, and I will rebuild the tent of David that has fallen; I will rebuild its ruins, and I will restore it, that the remnant of mankind may seek the Lord, and all the Gentiles who are called by my name, says the Lord, who makes these things known from of old.'*

James utilized Amos 9:11–12, applying it to the Messiah's return to rebuild the tent of David, meaning the kingly rule of his line, as promised in the Davidic Covenant (2 Sam 7:13). Jesus' reign from David's throne begins in a world with some people who do not know him. The remainder of the passage confirms the transitional millennial period in including the need for mankind to seek the Lord, precluding its fulfilment in the Eternal State (Rev 21:3).

1 Corinthians 15:23–26:

> *But each in his own order: Christ the firstfruits, then at his coming those who belong to Christ. Then comes the end, when he delivers the kingdom to God the Father after destroying every rule and every authority and power. For he must reign until he has put all his enemies under his feet. The last enemy to be destroyed is death.*

The apostle wrote on a stage of the kingdom that will begin after Christ's return and end when he has defeated all of his enemies, including death. This means that even after Jesus returns to reign, there will still be sinners and death in the world, just as the prophets foresaw (e.g., Isa 65:20). When the Kingdom of God is handed over to the Father it will be free of sin and death, identifying it as the Eternal State (Rev 21:4, 8). This is basic summary of future events, supporting the plain reading of Revelation 20.

Revelation 20:4–6:

> *Then I saw thrones, and seated on them were those to whom the authority to judge was committed. Also I saw the souls of those who had been beheaded for the testimony of Jesus and for the word of God, and those who had not worshiped the beast or its image and had not received its mark on their foreheads or their hands. They came to life and reigned with Christ for a thousand years. The rest of the dead did not come to life until the thousand years were ended. This is the first resurrection. Blessed and holy is the one who shares in the first resurrection! Over such the second death has no power, but they will be priests of God and of Christ, and they will reign with him for a thousand years.*

For the purpose of this exercise, consider just this one point from Revelation 20. There are two distinct mass resurrections bookending a one thousand year age. Even if the thousand years is only meant to identify a lengthy period, when is it supposed to take place? Since both resurrections occur along with or after the coming of Christ, then the period between them would, by definition, indicate a transitional age. There simply is no way to read this passage and deny the Millennium if the words are to have any real meaning.

MILLENNIAL DESTINY

Even after a brief consideration of a few verses, it is hard to escape Scripture's uniform anticipation of the Millennium. Not surprisingly, prophecies

pertaining to the Messianic Age are centered on the promises in the unconditional covenants to Israel being realized. Everything God intended for
Israel will come to pass, as she finds herself exalted over all other nations.
This is not because Israel is inherently superior, but because God keeps his
word. Everything that will be glorious about Israel in the coming kingdom
will reflect the source: Jesus the Messiah, King, and Lord. Once all of Scripture is considered, it becomes only too obvious that it will take the personal
reign of the Messiah for the kingdom in Israel to operate as God desired. If
the kingdom was to only manifest itself in a world free of unbelievers, then
Israel could never fulfill her destiny as a light to the nations, showing them
the way to the LORD.

Bibliography

Augustine. *The City of God*. Translated by Marcus Dods. Raleigh, NC: Hayes Barton, 2007.

Bonar, Horatius. *The Coming and Kingdom of the Lord Jesus Christ*. Edinburgh: J. Rutherfurd, 1849.

Calvin, John. *Institutes of the Christian Religion*. Translated by Ford L. Battles. Louisville, KY: Westminster John Knox, 1960.

Chafer, Lewis S. *Satan: His Motives and Methods*. Grand Rapids, MI: Kregel, 1990.

———. *Systematic Theology Volume 7*. Grand Rapids, MI: Kregel, 1976.

Constable, Thomas. *Dr. Constable's Notes on Exodus*. Garland, TX: Sonic Light, 2016. http://www.soniclight.com/constable/notes/pdf/exodus.pdf.

———. *Dr. Constable's Notes on Ezekiel*. Garland, TX: Sonic Light, 2016. http://soniclight.com/constable/notes/pdf/ezekiel.pdf.

Durant, Will. *Caesar and Christ*. New York: Simon and Schuster, 1944.

Fitzgerald, Allan D., ed. *Augustine Through the Ages: An Encyclopedia*. Grand Rapids, MI: William B. Eerdmans, 1999.

Fruchtenbaum, Arnold. *The Footsteps of the Messiah*. San Antonio, TX: Ariel Ministries, 2011.

———. *Israelology: The Missing Link in Systematic Theology*. Tustin, CA: Ariel Ministries, 1989.

Gentry, Kenneth. "The Meaning of the "Millennium."" http://chalcedon.edu/faith-for-all-of-life/the-eschatology-of-victory/the-meaning-of-the-millennium/

Gieseler, J.C.I.. *Text-Book of Ecclesiastical History Volume I*. Translated by Francis Cunningham. Philadelphia: Carey, Lea, and Blanchard, 1836.

Gribben, Crawford. *The Puritan Millennium:Literature and Theology, 1550–1682 (Revised Edition)*. Eugene, OR: Wipf and Stock, 2008.

Harnack, Adolf. *The Encyclopaedia Britannica*, Twentieth Century ed., s.v. "Millennium." 30 vols. New York: The Werner Company, 1901.

Hiebert, Edmond D. "Evidence from 1 Corinthians 15." In *A Case for Premillennialism: A New Consensus*, edited by Donald K. Campbell and Jeffrey L. Townsend, 234. Chicago: Moody, 1992.

BIBLIOGRAPHY

MacArthur, John. "Why Every Calvinist Should Be a Premillennialist, Part 1."http://www.gty.org/resources/sermons/90-334/why-every-calvinist-should-be-a-premillennialist-part-1

Mathers, Cotton, and Increase Mathers.*The Wonders of the Invisible World*. London: John Russell Smith, 1862.

McClain, Alva. *The Greatness of the Kingdom*. Winona Lake, IN: Moody, 2009.

Pate, C. Marvin. *Reading Revelation: A Comparison of Four Interpretive Translations of the Apocalypse*. Grand Rapids, MI: Kregel Academic, 2009.

Peters, George N.H. *The Theocratic Kingdom of Our Lord Jesus, the Christ, as Covenanted in the Old Testament and Presented in the New Testament*. New York: Funk & Wagnalls, 1884.

Roberts, Alexander, et al., eds.*The Ante-Nicene Fathers Volume I: The Apostolic Fathers with Justin Martyr and Irenaeus*. New York: Cosimo Classics, 2007.

———, eds.*The Ante-Nicene Fathers Volume III: Latin Christianity.*New York: Cosimo Classics, 2007.

———, eds.*The Ante-Nicene Fathers Volume VI: Fathers of the Third Century.*New York: Cosimo Classics, 2007.

———, eds.*The Ante-Nicene Fathers Volume VII: Fathers of the Third and Fourth Century.* New York: Cosimo Classics, 2007.

Ryle, John C.*Coming Events and Present Duties*. London: William Hunt and Company, 1867.

Schaff, Philip. *History of the Christian Church*. New York: Scribners, 1884.

Schmitt, John, and Carl Laney. *Messiah's Coming Temple: Ezekiel's Prophetic Vision of the Future Temple*. Grand Rapids, MI: Kregel, 1997.

Showers, Renald E. *There Really is a Difference! A Comparison of Covenant and Dispensational Theology*. Bellmawr, NJ: The Friends of Israel Gospel Ministry, 1990.

Spurgeon, Charles H. "Justification and Glory." *Metropolitan Tabernacle Pulpit* 11 (1865) 241–252.

———. "The Form of Godliness Without the Power." *Metropolitan Tabernacle Pulpit* 35 (1889) 301–312.

———.*The Sermons of the Rev. C.H. Spurgeon*. New York: Sheldon, Blakeman & Company, 1858.

Terry, Milton S. *Biblical Hermeneutics*. New York: Philips and Hunt, 1883 Reprint, Grand Rapids, MI: Zondervan, 1976.

Iliffe, Rob. "Newton's Life and Work at a Glance." http://www.newtonproject.sussex.ac.uk/prism.php?id=15.

Toussaint, Stanley. *Behold the King: A Study of Matthew*. Grand Rapids, MI: Kregel, 2005.

Wesley, John, and Charles Wesley. *A Collection of Hymns for the Use of the People Called Methodists*. London: John Haddon and Co., 1875.

Whitcomb, John. "The Millennial Temple of Ezekiel 40–48." *The Diligent Workman Journal* 2, no. 1 (1994) 21.

Wise, Michael O., et al., trans.,*The Dead Sea Scrolls: a New Translation*. Rev. ed. San Francisco: HarperCollins, 2005.